Henry Cooper's

Book of Boxing

Henry Cooper's
Book of Boxing

Arthur Barker Limited London
A subsidiary of Weidenfeld (Publishers) Limited

Published in Great Britain by
Arthur Barker Ltd
91 Clapham High Street
London SW4 7TA

ISBN 0 213 16842 1

Printed in Great Britain by
Butler & Tanner Ltd, Frome and London

Contents

Illustrations

Between pages 120 and 121

Between pages 152 and 153

Except where otherwise indicated, the photographs reproduced in this book were supplied by Syndication International Ltd.

Preliminary Round

I know that I am not backward at coming forward. I have never been frightened of getting up and having a go, and I admit, without having my arm twisted, that I can chat with the best of them. My public performances, these days, are expected to include a heavy helping of bonhomie. I have done more Dutch auctions than the Mayor of Amsterdam, and squirted more metaphorical oil on wheels than the Secretary-General of the United Nations.

I am not expected to be too serious. Yet I can be. You ask those boxing promoters with whom I and my old manager, the late Jim Wicks, did business. I have discovered that I can be a thinker of some depth – especially where British sport is concerned.

I always fought with a Union Jack in front of my eyes, and I'll still wave one, given any excuse. The chance to have a go at the knockers is rare, and this time I cannot be interrupted, so I'm coming out punching!

Actually, I'm a peaceful sort of guy. I've never thumped anybody in anger, not even the driver who carved me up and then pretended he wanted my autograph when I wound down the car window. I didn't bother to ask him how he recognised me through the tinted rear window of the Jag.

Nevertheless, the old knuckles do get a twitch on, especially when our lads and lasses don't receive the credit they are due. I'll tell you this, it is hard enough to succeed in world-level sport when you can devote twenty-five hours a day to it. Our boys and girls, particularly our amateurs, achieve miracles and then the Seb Coes and Steve Ovetts do the impossible for encores.

I hope British sport never gets involved in drugs, but world sport has a serious problem. So what's new? Nothing. It was rumbling about when I fought in the Olympics back in 1952. It was in Warsaw, round about the same time, that I was given the most strict medical I have ever had in my life, and sports medicine was supposed to be in its infancy then. If what we amateur boxers from Britain got from the Polish medico was infancy, all I can say is heaven help us when the child becomes an adult, because in the Eastern bloc countries the menace is still growing.

What they are doing, and have been doing for years, is an affront to the human body. If we can't beat 'em, we must never join them. But occasionally we can win – and do. What makes the achievements of Coe and Ovett so magnificent is that they beat people who have virtually been bred to run; whose physical development and diet have been programmed to their last yard of training, the last grain of rice.

Back in Warsaw, all those years ago, we had the treatment from a team of about eight specialists before and after we fought. We had our heads examined, with calipers. They thumped our chests, and dug fingers into our stomachs. They measured our arms and legs, and listened to our hearts. After the fights there were electro-cardiographs, brain scans ... I don't know what they didn't do. Our own doctors just told us to cough, to say 'ah', and pressed our hands. If we didn't wince, we were fit.

I don't know whether the Iron Curtain lads had computers then. They probably did. But they were learning from the finest specimens of British manhood and conducting an exercise that, multiplied a few thousandfold, provided data to help breed the perfect space-age man, no matter how they had to store it.

All the western world's science fiction is now not so far removed from the truth. Eastern bloc countries can measure children and calculate their height and build for future years. If they are going to be good for ballet training, for hurdling, or have the lung capacity to make a marathon runner, they can be channelled accordingly. Steroids, the drugs that caused all the fuss years ago, have become basic, almost old-fashioned. Drugs are so sophisticated these days that there is little chance of a scandal similar to the one that enveloped the Press sisters of Russia in the middle sixties.

Tamara Press won Olympic gold for putting the shot in 1960 and 1964. She was also the discus champion in 1964. Sister Irina left them all behind in the 1964 pentathlon. But there were hormone tests after the 1964 Games in Tokyo. There were suspicions about the Presses. Were they sisters? Or half-brothers? I have no idea, but I often wonder why their athletics careers came to such a sudden and mysterious end.

There are no drugs in British boxing, professional or amateur. For one thing it would be extremely difficult to calculate the dosage when it is not certain whether a bout will last one round or fifteen. But when I went to Moscow for the 1980 Olympics, I saw some astonishing sights. Middleweights, for instance, who had shoulders like heavyweights. They looked so strong I wondered how they were going to make the weights. They did though, and yet the arms and muscles were huge and they were very powerful about the body. Our lads - boys in their teens some of them - had skinny arms with hardly any muscle showing. I thought their opponents looked like monsters.

So abnormal and so coincidental, the development of muscle where it is wanted ... in the arms of boxers and in the legs and arms of gymnasts. Not even for the Union Jack would I ever want us to go all that way. There is a terrible price to pay. Remember little Olga Korbut, the Russian gymnast, who entranced the world when she won three golds and one silver at the 1972 Games in Munich? She was seventeen years of age then, but photographed eight years later she would have passed for forty.

We have, in Britain, some of the best raw material. Coe

and Ovett did it virtually off their own feet and I am delighted that the laws of amateurism have been relaxed sufficiently to permit the stars to generate income from their talent. It isn't right that they should have to struggle.

When I went to the Helsinki Olympics in 1952, I received nothing. In fact, it cost me money. I packed up work for six weeks before we left to concentrate on training. But not before the family had twisted my arm. I didn't like the idea of living off them for that time, but they said it was their gesture and they all chipped in. I was eating steaks, too.

What British sport does with the raw materials is marvellous. But while I cannot condone interfering with nature to the frightening degree that some nations are now doing, there is a happy medium, and Britain has to start doing a lot more in the field of sports medicine.

There is nothing wrong, either morally or any other way as far as I am aware, in speeding the recovery time after injury or in improving somebody's stamina or physique. But I did say improve, and not distort.

Medically, the British Boxing Board of Control is surely the most enlightened body in world boxing. Improvements in the running and organisation of boxing are never dramatic, but over the years the Board of Control have evolved a medical standard that makes the boxer safer in Britain than in any other country. I don't think we can go much further without wrapping them in cotton-wool. I'd say we have the right balance.

We look after our fighters better than they do in the United States. There is more wastage over there. More of their boxers end up in a bad way or drop out of the game after four or five fights than do ours. Many States still have the no-foul rule, which means anything goes. The rabbit punch and the kidney punches are illegal in Britain, but in the States you are given a minute to recover from either of those blows. A minute is a long time in boxing, but you have still been hit.

I also think our method of controlling a fight, with the

referee in the ring in sole charge, is far and away the best. Anybody can make a theoretical case for judges outside the ring. But in practice I don't agree.

Even with the best of views available, a judge at the ringside can see only threequarters of the fight. The action on the far side of the ring can be hidden from him by one or other of the fighters and also the referee. The far side of the ring is also usually twelve to fourteen feet away from him.

There have been some hilarious decisions at the Olympics, and at European title fights when, sometimes, the referee scores along with the judges. Two of the judges get it close and yet the third man is so far away, I wonder whether he has been watching a different fight. And that is the answer. He has seen only one boxer, the one he might have leanings towards.

There was a bit of that, I thought, at my one and only Olympic fight. I fought a Russian, Anatoli Perov. One judge came from France and the other two from Iron Curtain countries. I reckon I'd done enough to nick it. So did the Frenchman. But the Iron Curtain judges went for the Russian, and I was out on a split verdict.

Unlike the judges, the referee sees it all. He is never more than a couple of feet away from the boxers, and any blind side exists only momentarily. The man inside the ring should do it all.

The Board of Control run British boxing splendidly. One of the major factors in that happy state of affairs is the fact that none of the Stewards is financially involved in the game. So they can be independent and impartial. Nevertheless, I would like to see professionals on the Control Board, *without the power of vote.*

Who knows most of what is going on in boxing? The professionals. A whisper in a gymnasium in the North Country one day can be all round London the next. But that grapevine does not always include the Control Board officers.

I think administration would be so much stronger if a

promoter, a manager, a trainer and a boxer were called in to the Board's meetings, purely on a consultancy basis. Then the Board could be advised immediately of the feelings of the men who are in the game for a living. After all, it is they who should be considered first.

Jim Wicks and I tried to get this through on the Southern Area Council during my fighting days. The suggestion received some sympathy, but that was all. Eventually we stopped trying.

The Boxing Board of Control must take a technical knock-out in one area of their operations. They take pride in the fact that they are not in the game to make profit. That is good. But they should be, to a certain extent, and that is in respect of boxers' pension funds. When I was active in the ring, I looked after my financial future in several ways, including the buying of a pension, the normal practice of the self-employed businessman. But not all boxers were fortunate enough to earn the sort of money I did.

It doesn't rankle that when I was topping the bill, the Control Board took ten per cent of my purse. But I do wish they would have taken ten per cent of all boxers' and used the money to buy collective pensions.

The Stewards of the Control Board have access to some of the best legal and financial brains in Britain. I don't see why it shouldn't be possible for a young boxer to pay a sum of money into a fund that will ensure he has something to come when he retires. After all, if that sum was in proportion to what he had paid in, he would have a further incentive for trying to lift himself up the bill among the better rewarded bouts.

Why shouldn't the Control Board go to one company with the offer of a block deal? The bait of several hundred policies, pensions, annuities or whatever would surely tempt any assurance or finance company to offer advantageous terms.

It happens in other businesses. How else are company pension schemes and union pension schemes organised? The count of ten can often signal the onset of a boxer's long retirement. Surely the Control Board can beat it.

After all, boxing has been around a long time and it will, I am sure, be with us for many a year yet. It might be slightly different from the way we know it now. But look how different boxing is from what is was even fifty years ago.

I think the number of professional boxers will reduce. Boxers are far better educated than they used to be. Nobody fights today because he has to, which means that those who do put on the gloves have worked out their reason for doing so.

Most of them are aware, being realistic, that they have no chance of becoming champion of the world. Some might feel that the British championship is within their scope. But a surprising number will be thinking of four or five years, about twenty fights, to put together a bit of capital with which to buy a business. Boxing is not a game for going into with your eyes shut.

Why I got hooked on boxing is a story I will tell later. Nowadays I enjoy watching all sorts of sports. When I was a boy the other sport I really enjoyed was football. In fact I could easily have become a footballer. Without being bigheaded, I was a goalkeeper good enough to represent South East London schoolboys. How I came to be in goal I don't rightly remember. I suppose I did what I was told, as usual, but I assume that I was told to get in goal because I was a big fellow. Which reverses the accepted schoolboy process which sticks in goal the poor kid who is the least likely to argue about it – usually the smallest.

My hero then was a big red-headed goalkeeper who played for Charlton Athletic, whose ground at The Valley was about five miles from where I lived as a kid. Sam Bartram was a character. Big, athletic, and an entertainer. Including wartime friendlies, he played in more than a thousand first-class games and, I'll guarantee, gave the crowd something to laugh at in each one. In my book, he was the best goalkeeper *never* to play for England, and I counted it a privilege to enjoy his friendship when he became a Fleet Street sportswriter. Sadly, he died in 1981. They don't make players with Sam's outlook any more, which is a shame because the game needs them.

I agonised with the England soccer team during those palpitating qualifying games for the 1982 World Cup finals. It was that Union Jack business again. I'm prejudiced enough to think that because we invented soccer and gave it to the world, we should be king-pins. But nobody stays on the top by divine right. I didn't when I was British heavyweight champion, and it got harder as I grew older. But I stuck it until I was thirty-seven, grinding away to keep fit.

It is never again going to be easy for England. Nor West Germany. Nor Brazil. Nor any other team that has once been the best, for everybody wants to topple the champs. But West Germany survives, and I don't think the word slump translates into Brazil's language.

I'm fortunate enough to be able to make Wembley fairly frequently when England are playing there, and I must admit I get choked when I see them losing. It seems to me that we are no longer able to produce the players who can turn the half-chances into goals. To win anything at world level, of course, a country has to have the players who can turn quarter-chances into goals.

Most of the present players seem to come off the same conveyor belt. There are exceptions and one of them, and I make no apology, is my great mate Kevin Keegan. We have been known to make a splash together and have been well rewarded for it by an international company who think our faces sell their products.

Making television advertising films is not easy. Mistakes come expensive because budgets are tight and time is expensive.

But Kevin's attention to detail is enormous. His enthusiasm is tremendous and I'm not surprised that he twice became European Footballer of the Year – and also England's captain. Eleven Kevin Keegans would make a side capable of winning the World Cup twice over. The lads on the terraces have it right when they start chanting: 'There's Only One Kevin Keegan.'

English players cannot be criticised for lack of effort. They never stop running. Maybe that is part of the trouble. Running for ninety minutes doesn't produce flair. It is flair that entertains the crowd and, nine times out of ten, it is flair that wins matches.

I suppose if I could wrap up my ideal footballer and present him to England, I would have to call him Jimmy Greaves. Jimmy was everything I've been on about. He could run, when he had to. But that wasn't often because he could sense how a move should go and would see the opening almost before the ball was in it. Sweat was for other players. Jimmy had style, and I think it was a sad day for football when he revealed that the real reason for his retirement was that he had suddenly stopped enjoying the game.

I understand Jimmy, because he, on the east side of London, like me on the south, came from a working-class family, and with that background a love of football is almost instinctive. Rugby, golf and hockey were for the posher people, and huntin', shootin' and fishin' required a monocle and a Bertie Wooster accent. So during the winter, you either played soccer or you boxed.

Having an excess of sheer animal spirits to work off, I played both – and occasionally, I regret to have to reveal, managed to combine the two on the football pitch. But who didn't in those nostalgic days of coats for goal-posts?

I liked keeping goal. My schoolboy reputation must have gone on ahead of me when I went to work at Sydenham Gasworks because it wasn't long before I was filling the keeper's jersey in their first team. Working it out now, I would have been sixteen or seventeen with the amateur boxing career progressing nicely, too. How I found time for it all, I don't know, but eventually the soccer had to stop. I was getting some good-class amateur fights and moving steadily up the ladder.

I don't have a favourite football club, not in the sense of being an avid fan. But there is a close bond between me and Arsenal, and if they are doing well, then it makes me feel good, too. There are two reasons: the sentimental pull of having made my challenge for Muhammad Ali's world title on their ground at Highbury, and the debt I owe them that they will never allow me to try and repay.

Back in 1969, I collected the footballer's injury - while training for boxing. I did the cartilage on the inside of my right knee. It was straightforward, simple, and I was on my back for a fortnight after the operation. When I left hospital, the medical men suggested there was no better place to restore me to fitness than a football club. Somebody put a word in the right place and Bertie Mee, who was then Arsenal's manager and a physiotherapist himself, told me that he would be delighted if I would join them.

So I did. They laid out the red carpet, spared me little of the pain and anguish professional footballers go through, and restored about two inches of muscle wastage on my thigh. They told me they had been delighted to help and I was to regard myself as their guest. Arsenal are a big club in more ways than one.

Since I stopped playing football, I have never really indulged in two sports at the same time. There is still a hard, competitive instinct in me and I like to be good, or as good as I can be, at whatever I'm doing. When I became a professional boxer I decided that every other sport must go out of the window. I think the results justified my decision.

So I never played golf until I was near the end of my fighting career. Nowadays I'm disappointed if I don't get in at least two games a week. After all, I have to keep my swing grooved for all those celebrity pro-ams which people are kind enough to invite me to play in.

I think I must always have had an urge for golf – even as a kid. With my brothers – George, my twin, and Bernard, who is four years older – I used to be taken for the occasional day's outing to seaside towns like Margate and Cliftonville on the Kent coast. We always had a liking for the pitch and putt courses and the putting greens. I might have been a natural, but I never picked up a club, once I had started punching for a living, until I was thirty-five years old. I reckoned I was old enough to be in control of the situation when a pal of mine named Bill Finney invited me to Ealing Golf Club. How wrong can you get? I was bitten by the bug, and I reckon it will stay in my system until I take the long count.

I am not going to be drawn into an opinion whether I like golf better than boxing or vice versa. One became work and the other is total relaxation. The beauty of golf is that it is the greatest switch-off I know. You just cannot play it and think about anything else at the same time. You can't be got at on a golf course, and you don't take your telephone out there with you. It's peace in our time, and those people who smile understandingly and mutter about grown men hitting a little ball around the countryside just don't know the half of it.

I am not going to suggest that a love of golf hastened my retirement from boxing, but I did know that I probably hadn't more than a couple of decent fights left in me and I was beginning to calculate the amount of time I couldn't spend at the golf club.

Funny game, golf, especially the way I play it. I'm left-handed, and I haven't met a right-handed golfer yet who didn't think that all left-handers should have been put down at birth! I know we do everything the wrong way round. I know we look ugly. (I ought to apologise to every left-handed golfer in Britain, but I'm not going to.) I do everything left-handed except box. I suppose that is because when I first put my fists up, probably at about the age of six or seven, I automatically copied my Dad. Fighting southpaw – that's leading with the right hand – never occurred to me. I know a lot of left-handers who play golf right-handed because they started with right-handed clubs. There are so few left-handed clubs around that there is no chance of my ever winning a set as a raffle prize.

I must be the most totally left-sided person ever born. Everything I do comes from the left. I write left-handed. I lift a glass left-handed, but not very often. Boxing forced me to watch the booze. I like the occasional glass of beer, but prefer wine, and as far as smoking is concerned I'm still trying to recover from making myself sick with fags when I was about ten or eleven.

Tennis and cricket, as well as golf, I always played left-handed. When I was in my early thirties, I had a spot of trouble with my left arm. I had given the elbow a crack when I fell off my bike as a kid – I was probably trying to steer it right-handed! Anyway, they did all sorts of things to that elbow. The radiologist was busier than a seaside snapper. But when the doctors had finished eyeing all the X-rays they told me that the elbow showed the wear and tear of a bloke of seventy. We didn't say anything at the time, and got another five years of boxing out of it. Perhaps that is why only two of my last seven fights went the distance.

That elbow has never given me any trouble on the golf course, though Albina, my wife, does occasionally remark that it seems to stop me doing odd jobs around the house! I must say that I've always seemed to be able to hit a golf ball fairly well. The irons go fine, but I do have to be careful with the woods. To hit those screamers off the tee you need to have what golfers call fast hands. That means the hands give the club an extra whip when the head of it is coming into the ball. I just don't have fast hands – for golf.

Mind you, I do manage, if only very rarely, to belt the tee shot about 250 yards – straight out of the screws, as we golfers say. It sounds like the crack of a rifle, and the ball carries across the skyline for a long, long time. Every soaring second is ecstasy. For me, the feeling is the same as when 'Enery's

'Ammer, the old left hook, used to thump on somebody's jaw. The magic moment in boxing is when you see your opponent's eyes start to roll.

I could settle for the professional golfer's life. I would have loved to have been a Tony Jacklin, even with the pressures of having to putt with thousands of pounds or dollars at stake. In a situation when the result of a match is all down to me, even in one of our televised games when the audience can be vast, I don't feel all that much tension.

I appreciate that golf is not my living, but if you get to the top in any sport, then you learn to live with pressure. Golfers will tell you that the walk up to that final putt, with the difference in coming first or second measured in huge sums of money, can be the loneliest stroll in sport. You get pressure of a different kind in boxing. With me, it used to come before the fight. I was fine when the action started.

What the two sports have in common is that the man who can control his nerves is the man who will come out on top – or he will at least nine times out of ten. The boxer starts to feel the butterflies a week before any big fight, and an hour before the bout the tension can be tearing at your guts. But you mustn't show it. A golfer will jab at the putt. A boxer will go into the ring like a damp dishcloth.

I hope my golfing friends will not take offence, but there is another big difference between the two sports. The golfer knows that he isn't going to be hurt.

I like golf people. Basically, they are all nice guys – and honourable people. It is a game that puts a man, or a woman for that matter, on trust. If you want to cheat, the chances are you won't be spotted. But the code of conduct is so good, the stigma of being found out so great, that most golfers go to extremes to be fair.

Those celebrity pro-ams in golf have given me so much pleasure, and have allowed me to meet most of the top players. Tony Jacklin is a beautifully instinctive golfer who can sometimes manufacture shots out of nothing. Gary Player probably started with less natural talent than all his contemporaries, but has more dedication and determination than almost any sportsman in the world. Gary goes out on to a golf course always believing that he can win – until the last putt goes down. It is the attitude any successful boxer must have. Once he starts to entertain the idea of defeat, then the professional fighter might just as well pack up.

Brian Barnes is a man after my own heart. His golf is his business. His pleasure is angling. He is the first to admit that he would rather be on a river bank with a rod and line than face five hundred yards of rolling fairway. I suspect that Brian sometimes says it with his tongue in his cheek. At match-play golf, which is man-to-man, knock-out stuff as opposed to winning with the lowest score after everybody has played a round, or the same number of holes, he is one of the fiercest competitors.

In the 1975 Ryder Cup match, Brian beat Jack Nicklaus, the greatest of golfers, twice in the same day. His attitude to knock-out golf is exactly the same as a boxer's – it's him or me. That is why I think Brian and I are so much on the same wavelength.

Smashing blokes, the professional golfers. I owe them debts, too. Playing with them, I've had more free tips and odd 'lessons' than I've had hot dinners. I used to play off a handicap of seven, which is pretty good, but now I've started going up again. It has its compensations. Off seven, I was having to play out of my skin to hold a reasonable score, struggling in the week-end fun matches to save my money against the 16-handicappers who were roaring round with shots to spare. I'm certainly not forking out as much cash as I did!

I don't manage to see much cricket. Golf gets in the way. But I enjoy three or four days at the Test matches. I think cricket needs atmosphere. To go and watch county cricket with only a few hundred spectators in a ground that holds twenty thousand is no pleasure and, frankly, I'm surprised if the players get much from it. The most exciting cricket is the one-day match. You get a result and see plenty of strokes and runs. The Test matches generate their own excitement.

I suppose the cricketer I was closest to was Ken Barrington, who died while he was on tour with the England party in the West Indies in 1980. What a tragedy. Ken was a lovely guy, and a tremendously enthusiastic golfer. He used to hit a golf ball like he hit a cricket ball, but he was good at the game. We played in a lot of pro–ams together, mostly for the Lord's Taverners and in the Harry Secombe classic at Effingham.

Like me, Ken was a great waver of the Union Jack. So are the Bedser twins, Alec and Eric, who I've also seen a lot of on the golf course. It's easy to tell the difference between me and twin brother George, but I've never been able to tell Alec from Eric. So how many times thay have sent me up is their secret.

I suppose the reason I didn't become deeply involved in cricket is that I couldn't play it. George wasn't a bad batsman. I'd look a million dollars at the crease, but as soon as the ball came I never seemed able to get my bat at it. Sadly, stroke play wasn't my style. I was impatient and nearly always had a heave-ho at the ball. But I like the company of cricketers, and have been able to do my bit to help the lads who play for Middlesex, my adopted county, on various fund-raising occasions.

I have only once had the courage to venture on to a tennis court. It was while I was in the Army, and I found it harder to play than it looks. Knocking the ball over that net into the far corner seems simple enough, but I found it almost impossible.

My wife, Albina, and I were invited to Wimbledon several times while I held the boxing titles. Wimbledon is superb. We were escorted into the royal box, and at precisely four o'clock we were invited to take tea. Nobody runs at Wimbledon except the players. It is the real traditional English atmosphere: dainty sandwiches, china cups and all that, and totally divorced from all that cut-throat stuff on the courts.

Those visits to Wimbledon helped cement a friendship with Roger Taylor, the former British Number 1, who built a tennis complex at Val de Lobo in Portugal. I think Roger and I get on so well because we both had to claw our way up the ladder, me from the council estate in South London and Roger from the cobblestones and public park tennis courts of Sheffield. I hope people never forget that, in his playing time, Roger virtually carried English tennis on his back.

Like me, Roger is left-handed. Like me, he had his brushes with authority – I once resigned the British heavyweight title when the British Boxing Board of Control wouldn't back me for a world title fight against Jimmy Ellis, of the United States, while Muhammad Ali was having his dispute with the American military authorities over his call-up to fight in Vietnam.

But it was Roger who put Britain first when the professional tennis players ordered a boycott of Wimbledon in 1973, and Roger is the only Englishman to have reached the Wimbledon semi-finals three times since the war. I always try to meet him when I'm in Portugal, and I can beat him – at golf.

I was never tempted to have a go at rugby. I was ordered to play the game in the Army, and I quickly came to the conclusion that while I didn't mind getting into fights, I did like to know when they were supposed to start. . . . I did not want to get involved in those scrums. They were too dangerous for me.

I am no betting man. Jim Wicks had a lot of experience of that game. He had been in bookmaking and was always an enthusiastic punter. Danny Holland, who trained me for many years, followed the horses with the same concentration as he followed boxing. But with a conspicuous lack of the same success. With those two around me, I was never tempted to become a daily punter. But I do like a day at the races, and I am still delighted to do my stuff at the stable lads' boxing championships. Boxers and jockeys also have an annual golf match.

Even in the sixties, Jim would occasionally put £100 on a horse. I remember going racing with him one day, and he always took the mickey out of me because I would never pass the bookie more than a pound note. But this day, when Jim handed over seven tenners, I went barmy and had £5. Jim's eyes popped, and so did mine when I got back the best part of £40. Jim couldn't understand it when that forty quid went straight into my pocket and stayed there, but I suppose it gives an insight into the Cooper character. Because I grew up in a family for whom pound notes were as scarce as over-generous boxing promoters, I have never had any trouble appreciating the value of money.

Neither have I ever been tempted to own even a leg of a horse. Charles St George, one of Britain's leading owners, is a friend of mine. I'm a director of several of his companies. Charles has often asked me if I want a leg or a half-share, but I always tell him that I'll have all the fun of ownership by proxy – through him.

I don't pretend to know a lot about racing, except that it is expensive and, unless you get taken into top peoples' boxes, there isn't much comfort. I also know that both Jim and Danny lost fortunes.

That is why I am more likely to be at the Derby than any other race meeting, and I'll admit that it is largely because I have the contacts to be able to do it properly. The late Mirabel Topham, who owned Aintree, asked Albina and me up to Aintree for the Grand National. We stayed overnight, had a VIP escort round the jumps on Saturday morning, a champagne lunch and watched the racing from a private box. That is how to go racing – in style.

How the average punter puts up with conditions in the cheaper rings, I just don't know, and I'm not being snobbish about this. Being pushed and shoved all the time isn't either funny or fascinating, and I'm surprised British racecourses attract as many spectators as they do.

And then there is motor racing. I have always fancied that. But Jim Wicks and Jack Solomons, who promoted most of my early fights, would have torn their hair out. Fast cars have always turned me on, and I have always had a good motor. As a driver, I'm no madman – I'm too fond of my own skin for that. But when I see a nice road in front of me I do like to put my foot down.

Graham Hill, who won the drivers' world championship in 1962 and 1968 and was runner-up three times, was the most lovable character in British motor racing, until he lost his life piloting his own aircraft home from a meeting in the south of France. We were fairly close neighbours and great friends.

I have one especially vivid memory of Graham. I'd been asked to drive in a couple of celebrity races at the Brands Hatch track down in Kent. No way were we going to be allowed to go too fast – the cars would have been doctored, I suppose.

Graham, who was a great, great driver, said to me: 'Come down to Brands, I'll show you what it is all about.' It was an unbelievable experience.

There are two circuits at Brands. We went on the smaller one, in a modest vehicle – not one of those Formula 1 monsters. I climbed in with Graham, found something to hang on to, and within five seconds all my knuckles were white. What that genius could do with a car! The circuit was virtually all bends. Graham hardly ever dropped below a hundred miles an hour, and he didn't touch the brakes, as far as I could see. He was consistently in a controlled skid. The only thing I could smell was burning rubber. He knew what he was doing, every single second. And when we clambered out Graham said, without a trace of big-headedness: 'Trouble with those things is that they are so slow.'

I thought *I* could drive, but that was such an eye-opener

that I have never since been tempted to talk over-confidently about what driving skill I possess. The James Hunts of this world survive only because the ability to do so was born in them. No amount of tuition could make a man balance a car like they can.

I haven't had the Grand Prix urge since that drive with Graham. Now I am content to watch - with unbounded admiration for the boys in the big league and the seemingly unflappable way they do it.

But enough of me. The first bell is about to go. On to boxing. Let me tell you why I did it, how I did it, and what boxing is all about.

ROUND 1

Sport – or Stupidity?

Henry Cooper, millionaire. That would be me if I had a quid for every time I've been asked to justify the very existence of boxing. I've been told that it is barbarous. I've been told that it is an affront to the dignity of man. I've had my sanity questioned. But nobody has risked a left hook by suggesting that my brains are scrambled.

They tell me I've been good for boxing. That's not for me to judge. I do know that boxing has been good to me, and I get a reminder of that every time I pass a building site. If it hadn't been for boxing I could easily still be among the lads throwing the plaster up for a living. And home wouldn't be a handsome house with a swimming pool in the back garden. I know there are a lot more swimming pools around nowadays, but there aren't too many of them glittering in the sun when it shines on the South London suburb of Bellingham where I grew up.

Without boxing there would be no more games of golf with the celebrities which, as a life-style, is one I rather enjoy. No television performances that delight the ham actor in me. No more instant recognition. I may have big fists, but a big head I certainly haven't got, so I won't pretend that I don't enjoy all the acclaim that goes with being a personality. Of course I do. Who wouldn't?

All right, the cynics will argue, that is the pot of gold Henry Cooper has mined from boxing. The trappings of success wrested from the pain and anguish of others, with the size of the ante raised by the number of opponents supposedly shuffling around punch-drunk after taking batterings from 'Enery's 'Ammer.

Just let me say this. Nobody ever forced me into a boxing ring. Nor, to the best of my knowledge, were any of the men who felt the weight of my fists, made to fight. I still bump into a good many of them, from time to time, and far from being punch-drunk, there are those among them whose wits are sharp enough to make me think twice about sitting down in the same card school.

Then, there was the best reason of all, as far as I'm concerned, for boxing. I liked it. If my Mum and Dad had been against boxing, I have to admit that I wouldn't have been a very dutiful son. I like boxing, not because I want to inflict pain but because it satisfies one of the basic urges in a boy or man.

You are out there, entirely on your own, and you prove that you are top dog. You can do it with your own wits and your own ability. No help from a bat, a ball, a racquet, or even a club.

Naturally, I am aware that there is death in the ring. But in the thirty-five years following the Second World War, there were only nine fatalities in Britain, and three of those concerned foreigners whose countries may not have had the same high medical standards as ours.

Meanwhile people still fall off mountains. But there is no campaign to stop the climbing of Everest. Racing drivers and motor-cyclists lose their lives with alarming rapidity and, it seems to me, appalling inevitability. But the wheels don't stop turning.

Where boxing suffers in comparison to other sports is that when a tragedy happens on a field or a track it is always regarded as an accident. Boxing is never allowed an accident. Yet how can anyone seriously accuse boxers of getting into the ring with the intention of killing?

I wouldn't insult anybody who is against the fight game by suggesting their theories are nonsense. They are entitled to their opinion, and I to mine – which happens to be that physical danger is part of the lives of all of us and experiencing it doesn't do us any harm – in the long run. A man's body and brain respond to the adrenalin which danger generates.

I'm certainly not saying that a world war every generation would be a good thing, but I'm sure the human body is not a vegetable. If boxing is to be banned, we might just as well stop people driving fast cars or even playing soccer and rugby. As I see it, the risk factor is just as great.

Then there is the old argument about amateur boxing being sport and the professional side being business. I would never argue otherwise. But I say again, nobody ever forces a boxer to turn pro. Apart from liking the game, I also fancied the money, knew what I was doing, and reckoned I could look after myself.

I must have taken more ear-bashings on the subject of punch-drunkenness than I took fists in the face in all my fifty-five professional fights. That figure of fifty-five is important. It is about average for the modern boxer. I would never deny that the professional fight game can be brutal. I would never deny that punch-drunkenness used to be rife. But that was half a century and more ago, when a man could have between four and five hundred bouts.

The body cannot stand up to that sort of misuse, but in those days it was often a case of fight or starve, and with no other money coming in, the old-time pug would be slinging leather every week for the best part of ten years. Too often, the next fight would be on him before he had recovered fully from the last.

That situation just couldn't happen now. Supervision is extremely strict in most countries – especially Britain, where boxers who have been either knocked out or stopped are automatically suspended for three weeks. Their licences can be withheld for longer if the medical authorities are doubtful. There will be neuro-tests, skull X-rays, brain scans and cardiographs before they are permitted to resume fighting. The careers of professional boxers are monitored from start to finish. The tight check on the medical aspects of their careers means that if a boxer is taking too many defeats, he is dropped in class to a standard more suited to his talents, or is compulsorily retired.

Refereeing standards, too, are higher. Today's officials are better informed on the medical dangers. They know the signs to look for, and as soon as there is a reduction in a boxer's performance, they will step in and stop the contest.

Using statistics of sixty to seventy years ago to condemn boxing just isn't on, and I wonder how many of the knockers have ever been inside a ring. All this nonsense about pain should be taken with the proverbial pinch of salt. Even the knock-out doesn't hurt, and I should know.

Three of the best boxers of my time, former world heavyweight champions Ingemar Johansson and Floyd Patterson, and Zora Folley, all caught me with their Sunday punches. Ingo and I were fighting for the European heavyweight title in Stockholm when he caught me in the fifth round with the right-hander they used to call Ingo's Bingo. Down I went. But I was still groggy when I got up and the referee stopped it. Under European rules, it is in the record book as a knock-out. I'll tell you this. My pride was hurt more than my head. I was only twenty-three, but I fell for one of the biggest con tricks in the world. It was an open-air fight with the sun just going down. I allowed myself to be worked round until, momentarily, I had the sun in my eyes. I didn't even see the punch, but a few seconds after the end, I was as right as rain.

Zora Folley, who later fought Muhammad Ali for the world crown, did me in our return fight. I had upset the world rankings by outpointing him at Wembley in 1958, and three years later he came back again. This fight was significant, because it was the last time I trained at home. After that, it was always five weeks away from the comfort of home to a place where we could concentrate on the work. I had also been having a little trouble with my left arm and I knew even in the first round that I had every chance of being in trouble. However, I didn't reckon to cop it as quick as the second round – but I did. My chin got on the end of a short right and it was another touch of the good-nights.

Floyd Patterson had been the ex-world champ for four years when he came over to Wembley in 1966, but he was still a world-ranked fighter and nailed me with the best punch I ever took. It came, at lightning speed, in the fourth round. I didn't see it. I didn't even feel it. The film of the fight shows me falling flat on my face. I didn't get up, and when I woke up a few seconds later, I hadn't even a headache – as usual.

Johansson, Folley and Patterson, they all hit me fair and square on the chin with good rights, and didn't do me any more than momentary damage. The only other k.o. on my record book came when I met Joe Bygraves in my first title fight – for the Empire crown. I reckon I lost this before the first bell, because I weighed in at 13 st 13 lbs – the heaviest at which I ever fought. When Joe k.o.'d me in the ninth with a dig to the body, I just hadn't enough breath left in me to get up and beat the count. I was not pleased with myself and what I experienced on that occasion was more discomfort than pain. I put it down to inexperience, and I never made the same mistake again.

It is very difficult for the person who hasn't taken a punch to appreciate that pain in the ring is totally different to pain outside it. It is the difference between being caught 'cold' and 'hot'.

Let me put it like this. Imagine walking down a street with your mind on something else, and then bumping into a lamp-post. The clout will almost certainly bring tears to your eyes because the knock is totally unexpected. But when you are inside the ring you know you are going to be hit and all your concentration is on getting to the other fellow. It's a different situation entirely.

The blood is hovering around boiling point. Your mind is on tactics and targets and you feel you could punch your way through a brick wall. Unless the other fellow catches you with a belter, you hardly notice the punches landing. The aches and pains come later. Cuts need time to heal and bruises soon come out. I always used to have hot towels slapped on them straight after a fight. It never took me more than four days to look beautiful again!

Remember, too, that in boxing the assaults, for want of a better word, are planned. The accidents in other sports come when the body is braced for something else. Is it any wonder that they are more painful?

I knew a fellow who was a medical officer at the Royal Air Force College, Cranwell, during the Second World War. Somebody had the bright idea of banning boxing in case air crew were put out of action. Yet every weekend he could almost guarantee four broken noses – each the result of playing rugby.

In my book, the bodily-contact sport that carries the lowest risk factor is amateur boxing. The legendary Harry Mallin, winner of the Amateur Boxing Association's middleweight title five times and twice an Olympic champion, went through more than three hundred fights not only unbeaten, but unscathed as well. In his later years, there was no outward indication that he had ever been a boxer.

It was the same with Dick McTaggart, the Scottish light-welterweight who also added Olympic gold to ABA titles. He had more than five hundred fights, which doesn't suggest that mental and physical resources were being overstrained.

In the record books, too, is the name of Frank Duff, who was still entering the South West Division amateur championship at the age of forty-five.

Mind you, that shouldn't surprise anybody who knows his boxing, because 'ageless' Archie Moore, unquestionably one of the all-time greats, was claiming to be only that old when he was stripped of his world light-heavyweight title in the early sixties for failing to defend it. Archie was notoriously vague about his age. Most people in boxing, and his mother, too, reckoned at the time he was around forty-eight.

Mallin, McTaggart and Duff, and Moore in the professional game, are names that prove to me that boxing is not dangerous *unless* the fighter's ambitions are allowed to develop beyond his ability. Anybody who fights out of his class is asking for trouble. The amateurs find their own level, and wise professionals do the same. Or, if they take the advice a good manager should be giving them, they get out of the game.

There is no need for a boxer to be badly hurt or to suffer permanent disability. When the going gets tough, most fighters do the sensible thing and quit. Despite what the knockers of the game would have the rest of you believe, most of us don't have all our brains in our gloves.

Take my twin George. We turned pro together, but while I got on, he got out. He always cut worse than me, and we found that the bone underneath his eyebrows was sharper than mine. One decent punch in the wrong place and George would be streaming like a split tomato. The plastic surgeons took part of the bone away, but it didn't make a lot of difference. Wisely, George decided that enough was enough. He now runs his own contract plastering business, and is yet another boxer who has done all right by the game.

Alan Minter, the former world middleweight champion who, like me, started life as a plasterer, opened a restaurant and a leisure club in his home town of Crawley, in Sussex.

Tommy Farr, one of the three men (with Arturo Godoy and Jersey Joe Walcott) to take Joe Louis all fifteen rounds when the 'Brown Bomber' ruled the world with such style, finished his active business life doing big deals in paint and oil, a somewhat different life-style from his teen-age days in the Welsh mining town of Tonypandy in the dole-ridden early thirties.

Jack Petersen, who reigned as British light-heavy and heavyweight champion when the young Farr was climbing the boxing ladder, did well in the advertising business. His two sons and daughter were university-educated, and Jack later represented Wales on the Sports Council and became a Steward of the British Boxing Board of Control.

Dave Charnley, a fast-punching lightweight from Dartford, Kent, was British, Commonwealth and European champion and had two cracks at Joe Brown's world title in the early sixties. He developed extensive interests in building and property.

Boxing is not without its millionaires. George Walker, from London's East End, was the man who held the ABA light-heavyweight title before I won it in 1952. He turned professional with only limited success. Now, after a string of restaurants, garages, shopping complexes like the hyper-development at Brent Cross on the northern outskirts of London and a hotel in Cairo, there isn't a financier in Britain who doesn't welcome the sight of the Walker fist . . . wrapped round a pen poised above yet another business contract.

Neither is it true that all boxers were hungry boxers who fought out of need. Gene Tunney, who took the world heavyweight title off Jack Dempsey in 1926 and retired, ambition fulfilled, less than two years later, was born into the comfort of a New York family who never had to worry where the next few thousand dollars were coming from. He determined to become champion of the world and made it, though I dare say the million and threequarter dollars he made from three title fights came in useful. He also had the good fortune to marry a wealthy heiress. Their son became a United States senator.

If a man is going to fight, he is going to fight. The question of morality doesn't arise.

The history of boxing is illuminated with the names of men who owe the sport a debt in human terms. One of them was Johnny Owen, the Matchstick Man from Merthyr Tydfil, who paid his dues in full. He died in November 1980, a few weeks after being knocked out by Lupe Pintor when fighting for the world bantamweight title in Los Angeles.

Brave Johnny was twenty-four years old, a shy man who

lived in a world of his own. He had no interests other than boxing and his family. Girls, evenings out with the lads ... they were for other people. If backgrounds had not been there for the retiring Johnny to fade into, they would have had to be invented.

But boxing gave him an identity, authority and stature. He had twenty-eight fights, lost only two and drew one. Though he was British, Commonwealth and European champion, he was so modest that he never really came to terms with the fact that he was the most popular man in the boxing-steeped town of Merthyr. He could stand in any company and command the respect of those around him. But he wouldn't have been able to do it without boxing.

He died, not principally because the fists of the Mexican Pintor hit him once too often, but from cerebral bleeding after his head had hit the canvas. It was a freak injury of the kind that might happen to a footballer heading the ball the wrong way. Cerebral bleeding could happen to me if I stumbled off a pavement and struck my head on the kerb.

The life of Johnny Owen was tragically short. It achieved fulfilment because of boxing.

It could be, paradoxically, that one of the contributory factors in Owen's death was over-caution on the part of the Californian boxing authorities. I don't know, so I cannot point the finger. But I have noticed in Britain, in deference, I suppose, to public opinion, a growing tendency towards the over-protection of boxers. The floors of rings have become too well-padded and the eight-ounce gloves have been made compulsory for the heavier men.

When I was fighting, I much preferred the rubber under the canvas floor of the ring to be as thin as possible and not, as urged by all those people who fear head injuries when a boxer is knocked down, as thick as possible. Anybody who has boxed will agree with me.

Let me explain. There isn't a boxer who didn't want to be able to move his feet as quickly as he could, either to take avoiding action when in trouble or to exert the maximum leverage when wanting to attack. On thick rubber, the boxer's feet do not come out as easily as he would like and he isn't moving as fast as he wants. Given a firmer surface, the feet will virtually slide over the canvas.

So it could be argued that if Johnny Owen, who was a more than useful mover, had been fighting on a surface that was harder, then he might have avoided, or partially avoided, the blow that put him down in the twelfth round. I don't know. But I would certainly rather have fought on a concrete floor than a mattress.

I am the first to concede that the professional boxer is a bad risk. My insurance premiums dropped faster than if I'd hit 'em with the old left hook when I announced that I was retiring. So I have every sympathy with boxing authorities. The first duty must be the protection of the lads who provide the action. But I do think at times they have overdone it.

I have already mentioned the business of thickening up the ring rubber. I don't go much on that, nor on the eight-ounce glove. When I turned professional back in 1954, gloves were six ounces all the way up the weights. But since I have finished, middle, light-heavyweights and the big boys have to carry half a pound on each arm. Quite apart from the boxing, think how fit a fellow has to be just to carry that lot on the end of each arm for the hour that a 15 rounds title fight can last.

Seriously, though, this is a case of over-protecting the fighter without having sufficient thought for his opponent.

I have already said that each time I was knocked out cleanly I got up smiling. Had I been christened Mickey Finn, I couldn't have gone out quicker or more painlessly. But the trouble with eight-ounce gloves is that it is more difficult to knock somebody out than when wearing six-ounce gloves.

Before the hands go up in horror, before I'm damned for being an advocate of brutality, think about it. Imagine being in the ring with me. I'm going to thump you anyway. But with, say, four rounds to go, I've got you in trouble. With six-ounce gloves I can probably put you out of your misery with one punch you probably won't feel. Or with eight-ounce gloves I might need to land about twenty solid blows before you either go down or the referee steps in.

It isn't one punch that does the most long-term damage. It is the absorbing of punishment. I never want to see, and nor does anybody else in his right mind, a bemused boxer taking punch after punch.

Every blow to the head must damage the brain. That applies in any walk of life. When the motorist bangs his head on the garage door getting the car out, it damages the brain, even though it provokes no more than a rub and a swear word. Repeat that slight accident a thousand times in a non-boxing lifetime and there is no permanent damage. But the brain has still been bounced in its protective liquid and bumped against bone.

The boxer is of course committed to receiving more bangs on the nut than your pen-pushing neighbour, and I emphasise, yet again, that it is his decision. Yet do we have to make it harder for him by forcing his opponent to wear gloves that increase the chances of his soaking up punishment?

One of our leading experts in the field of sports medicine is Dr John Williams, who runs the Farnham Park Rehabilitation Centre at Slough and has spent a lot of time researching the effects of blows to the head, in all sport.

He is a good friend of mine, so I don't raise a fist even in mock anger when he suggests that the reason I didn't take much punishment in an amateur and professional career that spanned more than twenty years is that I cut so often.

I'll kill this myth even if it takes me a lifetime. Of the fourteen fights I lost, only four of them, including the two against Muhammad Ali, were stopped because I was bleeding. But I take John's point, even though I reckon I was pretty good at defending myself.

John would be happy, from a medical point of view, with

a nylon knuckleduster. He argues that it would at least teach boxers to punch properly. I don't know that I would go all the way with that, but when you examine the motives, John's is not all that outrageous a suggestion.

Certainly, the boxer whose hands are covered by only the minimum of protection would think twice before throwing a punch unnecessarily – as they did in the bare-knuckle days. There is a tendency now to regard that era of boxing as barbaric. That is a matter of opinion, but what is a matter of fact is that because of the risk of a boxer hurting himself, fewer punches were thrown. The big one didn't go in until the deliverer of the blow was virtually assured of hitting the target.

I know that the eighteenth- and nineteenth-century pugilists took some dreadful beatings, but that was because most contests then were fought to a finish ... twenty and more rounds being commonplace. John Williams reasons that with today's shorter fights – usually only title bouts exceed ten rounds – far less damage would be inflicted on the loser because he would take fewer punches. It would put the premium, John says, on skilful defence.

I wouldn't go that far. Attack is the name of the game, and I wouldn't want to see the character of the sport changed. What have we got if boxing is not aggressive? But John Williams and I, medical expert on one side and hardened old pro on the other, have this in common – we don't see the validity of eight-ounce gloves.

In boxing, as in everything else, keeping a sense of proportion is important. It will surprise the uninitiated to know that only about one blow in ten lands on the head or trunk. The majority, particularly opponents' left leads, are slipped or taken on the upper arms. Furthermore, despite all the charges of legalised mayhem, no more than one in every forty fights ends in a knock-out.

In life, we achieve nothing without risks. The pen-pusher takes one every time he changes his job. True, he is not subjected to violence, but if we have to have violence – and fighting is an animal urge – then boxing controls the amount of risk.

Let's go back to where we came in. The comfortable standard of living that I now enjoy, I owe almost entirely to boxing. Boxing is a superb character-builder. It taught me to eat properly, and it taught me that being a gallivanting playboy has no future. There was no point in boxing if I didn't give it a hundred per cent. Consequently, I learned that it is not a bad idea never to give less than ninety-nine per cent to anything I do.

That philosophy is acquired, I am sure, by all the lads who take up boxing seriously, and that includes the vast majority who have no intention of making a professional career of it. The average boxer joins an amateur club between sixteen years of age and seventeen and stays for about five years. Then marriage and the setting up of a home inevitably take over.

By then, the boxer will have assimilated good habits that will last him a lifetime. Boxers are probably the fittest of all sportsmen. They have to be, and the fitness kick has stayed with me. I certainly don't go road running any more, but I can still give the younger fighters a run for their money with the skipping rope.

Like most former boxers, I find keeping an eye on my diet no trouble. It is more than second nature. It is a lifetime's habit. I know that a combination of drink and poor nutrition dulls the brain cells, and consequently I have no trouble in living what I would call the clean life.

That doesn't mean I have a season-ticket to a monastery. It means that if I have a rich meal, I am most likely to skip the next one. If social circumstances demand three or four lagers, I will enjoy them without trying to become the brewer's best friend. I like wine with a meal. But a couple of glasses will do.

Not that all that keeps me completely out of trouble. I once had to postpone a fight because of an attack of gout. That was a real humiliation. Heavyweight champion of Great Britain, Europe, and the Commonwealth, and one of the fittest men in the world, k.o.'d by the pheasant and port wine disease.

It was only a twinge, I thought. I started taking the tablets, and the gout went away. I fought the fight good and won, and carried on taking the tablets. Down through the years to the end of my fighting days and beyond, it was one of my best kept secrets. But the cover was blown after the Open golf championship of 1981.

I was invited down to Sandwich for the last two days. Near the end of a very good meal, mine host served summer pudding without my realising that strawberries were in it. At the end of the meal, I was offered port. Carried away by the sheer pleasure of having seen most of my favourite golfers in action, I dropped my guard and accepted a port, on the condition that it was flyweight size.

That small port and a hint of strawberry did what the best heavyweights in the world had failed to do ... put me out of circulation for a fortnight. And I'm still trying to live it down.

Generally, thanks to boxing, I have no trouble in keeping on the straight and narrow. But, even though I doubt whether I can give back to the game what it has given to me, I would never force any lad into it. My own sons have never shown any inclination to become boxers. They played soccer and rugby, despite my telling them that more people have to pack up those sports with leg injuries and torn muscles than ever have to quit boxing.

When I hear boxing accused of being a sport of intimidation, I wonder what has happened to our beautiful game of cricket. I haven't yet seen any boxers having to wear helmets.

I'll leave the last word on the morality of boxing to a very great friend of mine, the late Arthur Dickson Wright, the eminent neuro-surgeon and boxing enthusiast. Arthur used to tell the ban-boxing brigade that he had seen very few head injuries among boxers . . . that he had seen far more as a result of domestic quarrels. And then he'd gently ask: 'So, shall we ban marriage?'

ROUND 2

Learning to Box

As a boy I never got any black eyes. My nose wasn't broken, though as noses go mine might even have been improved by a little pugilistic re-shaping. I never ran home to Mum with handkerchief soaked with tears because some bully had put one – or two or three or four – on me.

I was no better nor any worse than ninety per cent of red-blooded young ruffians. The urge to fight was primitive. But the schoolboy Cooper could look after himself long before he had grown out of his short trousers. Because I had been taught to box.

To most kids growing up in the forties on that council estate at Bellingham, fighting came naturally. After all, our fathers and elder brothers had been at it with the Germans and Japanese for years.

But boxing is different to fighting. Fighting is all hot blood, swinging fists and with the pain of taking three punches forgotten if you land two. Boxing is about discipline and keeping cool, and in Britain most youngsters can begin learning to box as early as nine years of age – particularly if, as in my case, there is a visiting fireman handy.

My twin brother, George, twenty minutes younger than me, fought professionally under the name of Jim because there was another George Cooper around at the time we started. My brother was a useful heavyweight who had to retire early in the mid-sixties because, as I mentioned earlier, his skin was cutting too often.

George and I were natural boxers. It runs in the family. My father's father, another George, fought bare-fisted and gloved, round the Elephant and Castle area at a time when, if you couldn't look after yourself, you struggled. Well, everybody in that area of London just before the First World War struggled, but Grandad George, who died at sixty-one when he burst a blood vessel singing, struggled less than most. They employed him as a bouncer at the old National Sporting Club when the legendary Jack Johnson, then the world heavyweight champion, was threatening to go into the club and take it apart because it was being put about by some of the aristocratic members that Jack had ducked a fight there.

I like to think that the old chap's reputation had got to Johnson. The most unpopular world champion of all time turned and left when Grandad asked him, politely, to leave. I often wonder what passed for politeness in the Elephant in those days.

My father, Henry William, spent six years in the Royal Artillery just after the First World War, and polished his boxing skills there, so it is easy to see where George and I got our enthusiasm for boxing.

There was a grass verge outside our house at 120, Farmstead Road, Bellingham. George and I would spend hours out there, when we got home from school, sparring with socks rolled over our fists for gloves.

One of our neighbours was a chap named Bob Hill, who had done a bit of boxing for the Fire Brigade. He suggested that we went with him over to Bellingham Boxing Club at the local British Legion hall. It was a rough wooden building with a pine floor. Gone now, but that was where it all started.

It is no more difficult to learn to box now than it was in those days. The Amateur Boxing Association has more than a thousand affiliated clubs; there is boxing in the schools; and there are the hundreds of National Association of Boys' Clubs. I reckon there must be about forty thousand boxers in Britain, and most of them will have started the way George and I did. It is the best way.

I am not saying the youngster isn't going to get hurt, but

what I am talking about is momentary pain. Youngsters are too closely supervised to suffer any serious damage, except possibly to their pride.

Bob Hill took us down there, and for a year we did nothing but learn the routines and absorb the atmosphere. Though I wasn't allowed to hit anybody, or be hit, I loved it. Kids today will be taught the same way as I was, by men who love the sport of boxing, have done quite a bit themselves, and have adopted boxing as a way of life. Practically all the work in an amateur boxing club is done on a voluntary basis.

Every amateur club has a number of trainers, but there is usually one who lays down the main pattern for the place. Ours at Bellingham was Matt Wells, at one time lightweight champion of Britain. He laid the foundations, and it was largely down to him that, at fifteen, George and I were able to climb the amateur boxing ladder and join the Eltham and District Club - then, as now, one of the leading clubs in the country.

But, as starry-eyed nine-year-olds, George and I were taught to skip, how to move our feet, how to punch and, more important, how to dodge punches, or to ride them. This is most important because boxing, basically, at the lowest level, has to be more of a defensive technique. No trainer, I can assure all the anxious Mums and Dads, is going to let their son inside a boxing ring until he has proved outside it that he has mastered enough of the rudiments of the game to protect himself.

Outside the ring, most boxers can hold their heads high, because there is no better sport for developing self-respect or earning it from others. But the novice boxer is soon taught that inside the ring, he buries his chin, fights with his eyes looking upwards and, in amateur boxing, with the hands held higher, right up in front of the face, than in the professional game. The punch-for-pay men, wanting extra power in their attacking blows, carry their fists lower. But that is all in the future for the novice.

It is a fact of boxing life that, at boyhood level, there is a high fall-out rate. Perhaps it is not surprising. It is not every boy who can buckle down to the self-discipline that boxing demands. We had a lot of fun at Bellingham, and later at Eltham when school days were behind us, but skylarking in the gym and all that sort of thing was out. Too many of us wanted to learn, and the trainers quickly showed the jokers the door.

I could have lived down at Bellingham Boxing Club. Gradually, I mastered the techniques, and after months of throwing punches at pads on the trainers' hands, and more at the heavy bag and speed-ball, I was allowed inside the ring with a carefully picked opponent.

Amateur club trainers keep a very wary and expert eye on how fast, or slowly, their boys develop. There is no danger of mis-matches at this level, and the length of time in the ring is rigorously controlled. At this stage, the boys are sparring under supervision rather than boxing. No trainer wants a lad's confidence to suffer as a result of finding himself out of his depth. But when one of the boys starts to get a bit above himself, the trainer has to do something about it. And Matt Wells did.

I was always a big lad, and maybe I was finding it coming a little too easy. One day Matt lined up the boys and picked a skinny one for me. What I had coming to me was a lesson in self discipline, but I didn't know it then.

I thought I would have a go. I did, and got a whole lot of leather in my face. Jimmy Tippit, as I found out the hard way, was the best boxer in the club. It was jab . . . jab . . . jab . . . jab . . . all the time, and after that I never ever went into any ring with over-confidence. Boxing fences are not to be rushed at. Even Don Quixote, one of the best fighters to come out of Spain, learned the hard way. Jimmy Tippit later became a professional at light and welter weights. I wasn't surprised.

I reckon most clubs will lose something like seventy-five

per cent of their original intake of nine-year-olds. Those that are left form something of an élite corps. Go into any club of reasonable stature on a training night and you will find upwards of fifty boxers, ages ranging from nine through to nineteen and upwards, but the older lads will be in a tiny minority by then. Boxing is basically a young man's sport, and unless he has turned professional, the average boxer finds that the demands of marriage, mortgage and parenthood, make too many inroads on his time. But there are the dedicated club boxers who, when their competitive days are over, will still go down to the club for exercise and good company. It is from characters like these that the young boys will learn.

Learning to box is not expensive. Boys need only a singlet – it is against amateur rules to box without one – shorts, socks and training shoes. The rest of the equipment, which is the stuff that doesn't come cheap, is provided by the club. Fellows like Bob Hall are the salt of the earth. When George and I first went down to Bellingham, the subscription was half a crown a year. That was one eighth of a pound – twelve and a half pence now, but it seemed a lot of money at the time. Bob paid the subs for both of us.

The ring, punch-bags, speed-balls and all the other bits and pieces needed to make the average boxing club go round, are provided by voluntary effort, with mums and sisters, wives and daughters doing the refreshments etc, and the income from staging some six or seven tournaments a year. If any youngsters' parents are having trouble with the subscription, then I know of no club, assuming the lad has already given evidence of his keenness, which will not divide the subscription into monthly, weekly or even nightly amounts.

Boxing is like that. I think it is shameful that there is such a great divide between the amateurs and the professionals. It is, regrettably, difficult for old professionals to give something back to the game. I would like to see the barriers broken down completely.

A few years ago, with a company sponsoring the events, we ran a series of tournaments for the Henry Cooper trophies. Yet, sometimes, I wasn't even allowed in the ring to present them. I am grateful to amateur boxing, of course, but that sort of attitude is ridiculous. Amateur boxing could receive so much more from the professional game but the suspicion still exists that we old pros might taint the young lads.

It is an attitude of mind I cannot understand . . . not while the amateur authorities are prepared to grant, as they do, around a hundred licences a year to old professionals to coach amateur clubs.

Most amateur clubs invite local businessmen and successful tradesmen to become vice-presidents. They are the obvious means to the obvious ends. They will make contributions to the club's welfare, either in cash or kind.

If I were a successful estate agent or legal man or involved in medical fields, I would like to assume that whatever I could offer the amateur game would be welcomed without any conditions.

But though I can claim to be successful in public relations, broadcasting and even as an underwriter with Lloyds, the most respected insurance organisation in the world, I am also Henry Cooper, ex-professional boxer, and as such I suppose people must feel that my motives might be suspect.

John Conteh, Terry Downes, Alan Minter, Maurice Hope, John H. Stracey, Ken Buchanan, Jim Watt, Cornelius Boza-Edwards and Walter McGowan are all Britishers who have become world champions since the early sixties. They could be an inspiration to young boxers. It is ridiculous to doubt their ability to impart boxing knowledge, and to allow them to contribute no more than coaching or the occasional handing over of a piece of silverware is surely an affront to their dignity.

But whether the youngster in the gym is guided by old professionals or the honest old amateurs for whom boxing is meat and drink, he will be quickly told that the first essential is the protection of his head. It is all right for the professionals to fight with their guards just in front or even below their chins. By that stage, they are in the game for money. It is part, if not all, of their livelihood, and it is their decision that they take risks. The high guard gives any boxer a better opportunity of sticking out a straight left to the opponent's head, and that is the punch that scores points. In the amateur game, of only three rounds, not more than twenty per cent of bouts end in knock-outs. The way to win is by points.

Nobody scores without a correct punch, and it was at this stage of my initiation into the rights and wrongs of the game that I was taught how to use the knuckle part of the fist to greatest effect. Then, I was taken on to the punch-bag. Nearly every amateur club I have visited looks like an obstacle course during 'working hours'. Bags swing gently from every rafter. I know the heavy bag cannot hit back, but it does not provide a rigid stationary target, which would be useless. Its swaying ways can be countered only by footwork, and that is developed through use of the skipping rope.

I received the skipping message loud and clear. I had realised by the time I was eleven that there was no better aid to developing mobility round the ring. Remember that I was always a big bloke, even at that age.

I soon cottoned on to the fact that unless I cultivated the secret of moving smartly, I was going to get hurt hard, and often. At our school only the girls skipped, but George and I were big enough to deal with anybody who called us cissies, so out came the ropes. At the start, I found that three or four hops on one foot was easiest, and then a change to the other foot. Gradually you sort it all out, and proficiency comes, faster than you think.

When I was training for the big professional fights, with so much at stake, I could skip without a break for a quarter of an hour. Even now, I find it a good way to deal with the superfluous ounces before they become pounds, but the only audience I permit are the family.

Matt Wells and his trainers wouldn't allow us in the ring until we could do our stuff with the rope. I reckon, and so did he, that anybody who could keep a rope going for a minute and a half had acquired the speed of foot needed to box properly. This is about the time, too, when a trainer puts the large pad on his hand and holds it at different levels and distances, inviting you to punch it while on the move. If the trainer is satisfied at this stage, the youngster is almost ready to go into the ring against an opponent. But not quite.

In my day he would have been, but now – to emphasise further how well boxing looks after its fighters' welfare – no youngster can duck through the ropes without producing a letter from his doctor certifying his fitness to enter a ring. Mums and Dads have nothing to fear.

Our Mum had only one fear and that was that George and I might be forced to fight each other. She wasn't exactly anti-boxing, but she would never go and see us fight. Later, on my big fight nights, she would have the radio on for the running commentary, but she wouldn't settle and listen. She would be in and out of the room, doing something else, or finding some household chore, but saying each time she passed the radio: 'How's he doing then. Is he all right?'

The chances of the Coopers being in the ring together were virtually nil. Boys from the same club are not allowed to box each other unless they are drawn together in an open championship.

Eventually, after a couple of years at Eltham and District Boxing Club, I graduated, at seventeen, from youth to senior ranks, and by then I was vastly experienced in open events. I had also acquired a medical card, which I had to keep throughout my amateur career of 84 senior fights, of which I won 73 and lost 11. The card has to be produced before every show when, once again, the boxer is examined before he enters the ring.

If an amateur boxer is knocked out by a blow to the head, he is automatically suspended. It used to be for twenty-one days, but now it is twenty-eight. I never received the automatic suspension, and not many do. Failing to beat the count is one thing, but it is rare for an amateur to be rendered totally unconscious.

Mind you, there are amateur fighters who build a reputation for putting their opponents away. It was defeating one of them that convinced me that I had better turn professional.

Tony Madigan was an Australian who came to England with the specific aim of winning an ABA title. In 1953 we clashed in the light-heavyweight final. I had managed to stay down to light-heavy to keep out of George's way. He was a natural heavy, so if I boxed in the lower division, we could enter the same open events without any chance of us meeting.

I had won the ABA title the previous year, but that didn't bother Tony, who stopped every opponent he met on the way to the final, a feat which is as rare in the ABA championships as an unseeded player winning Wimbledon. Tony had a punch like a kangaroo's tail, but I snatched the verdict on points and convinced myself that when I was out of the Army I would turn professional.

It was a decision I made with a certain amount of regret, but like many others before and since, I discovered that I couldn't live on chandeliers and cake stands. I had been taught plastering, an occupation that increased the strength in my natural left side and made its own contribution to the power of 'Enery's 'Ammer. But that was all I had.

George made the same decision to turn professional. Most successful amateur boxers, who win their silver spoons as distinct from being born with them in their mouths, make the same decision. There are one or two like Dick McTaggart, the Olympic gold medallist in Melbourne in 1956, and Nicky Gargano, three times ABA welterweight champion from 1954, who had other careers mapped out for them. But for most it was an obvious decision, taken not too reluctantly. There was no room for regrets. The circumstances didn't allow for any.

What I missed was the 'family' atmosphere of amateur boxing. Being a professional is a lonely life. It has to be. I soon realised that I wasn't part of a team any more. No more familiar faces at our three nights a week and Sunday morning training sessions. No more sing-songs on the way back from a club trip. No more the aggravation of journeys abroad where, although I was naturally proud to fight for my country, there was no time, because of the lack of finance, to do any more than get there as late as possible, fight, and then nip back home.

I went to Helsinki, for the 1952 Olympics, to Spain, to Germany, to Poland and other countries, too, without seeing any more of them than airport, arena and hotel. We did, in Poland, once get taken to see the Russian ballet. But with all due respect to Rudolph Nureyev and the other lads and lasses of his profession, I can't recall that particular trip doing anything for my cultural standard.

Had I kept all the silverware I won while boxing as an amateur, I would need a bigger house. There is some of it still at home, and I see quite a lot when we go visiting the relatives. It saved me a pound or two in wedding presents, and just before each Christmas we used to have the relations round and let them take their pick.

Silverware was the salvation for George and me when we were in the Army. There was a lot to be won there – a tournament every other week, it seems to me now. We did a deal with a staff sergeant and, for a small consideration, he used to take the stuff into the sergeants' mess and raffle it. Well, when you're on no more than three quid a week. . . .

The end of the amateur boxing road can be as near or as distant as any youngster likes to make it. It doesn't have to be the preparation for a professional career. There is a lot of pleasure to be gained, even if a youngster rarely boxes outside his own club.

Knowing that he can look after himself does a lot for any youngster's confidence. I didn't even lose mine when I discovered that the Company Sergeant-Major of the first battalion I ever joined was a fellow I had knocked out when he fought for his club against Eltham a couple of months earlier!

ROUND 3

A–Z of Ringcraft

ATTACKING Mostly done by the leading hand – the left in the case of boxers using the orthodox stance, and the right in the case of southpaws. The outstretched arm and fist combine to produce a punch that, ideally, travels straight from the shoulder. If, at the same time, the body turns, then more power is imparted to the blow.

More often that not, the target for the traditional straight left is the head. The straight left is always a punch that scores points for finesse. Should it get through an opponent's guard, and is timed correctly to strike the head just before the arm is fully extended, the effects can be quite dramatic and, occasionally, stunning.

The leading hand can also be used to land punches in the area of the solar plexus, the nerve centre of the stomach just below the ribs.

This does not mean that the right hand, or the southpaw's left, is used purely as a defensive weapon. Thrown across an opponent's left lead and at his jaw, it can be a fight-finishing punch. Used under an opponent's left lead to land in the area around the heart, it invariably places a question mark against his stamina.

Those are the punches which can be said to open the door. Once at close range, there are a variety of blows that can best be described as explosive, because each, properly executed, carries the threat of a knock-out.

'BREAK' The call by the referee to separate boxers who have become hopelessly entangled in a clinch. Neither boxer likes to make the first move towards creating more space between himself and his opponent, for the simple reason that he might be punished, painfully, as he retreats with fists lowered for a vital second or two, before being restored to the guard position.

When the referee calls 'break', both boxers have to step away from each other. Neither is allowed to launch a blow until the referee calls 'box on', the rule thus safeguarding both fighters.

COUNT It comes from the time-keeper outside the ring and lasts ten seconds. If the stricken opponent is not able to get up and defend himself, then his opponent is the winner. The time-keeper counts audibly, and the referee, standing over the fallen fighter, counts in unison for the benefit of the boxer. In official parlance, the boxer who fails to rise is 'out of time'. 'Knock-out' was a phrase coined by early boxing journalists and carried into common use.

DEFENCE Though points are won for attacking, the art of defence is no less important. If it is not mastered, then fights are lost. The best form of defence is the use of the ring, a skill developed through experience. Defence can be best appreciated by watching a good boxer taking evasive action after being knocked down. He will retreat to the outer areas of the ring while still feeling the effects of the blow. This forces his opponent to come forward and offer himself as a target for points-winning punches such as the straight left, hook and uppercut.

Defence means also guarding the most vulnerable points of the body. These are generally accepted to be the areas below the ribs, around the heart, the solar plexus, the temples, the edges of the jawbones and, of course, the chin.

EYES Let me end a myth. It isn't eyes that cut, it is skin. I had a reputation for suffering from cut eyes. It was all wrong. As I pointed out earlier in this book, I lost only four fights through cuts, but because two of them were against Muhammad Ali, the thing has been blown out of proportion. Usually, my cuts were in the same place, just above my leading eye – the left. If the cut is over the eye or in the eyelid and won't stop bleeding, the fight just has to be stopped for the basic reason that the boxer cannot see when blood is seeping into the eye. Because of the size of the glove, the only way eyes can get damaged is illegally. Take it from me, thumbs can be stuck in them and, yes, it is painful.

FIST A fist is made by clenching the hand so that the tips of the fingers are tucked into the palm. Everybody knows that, but if the fist is made properly then the rear part of the fingers are almost at right-angles to the back of the hand. The fist is square, box-shaped, hence the origin of the word boxing. The correct way to hit is by using the knuckle part of the fist.

GLOVES Made of leather with resilient foam padding. In the days before man-made fibres the filling was horse-hair. Amateur boxing regulations stipulate that the leather weighs no more than four ounces and the foam not less than four ounces. Gloves are always tied at the wrist with the knot at the back of the hand, and there is a bar across the palm to aid the grip. Professional boxers use gloves of six ounces between the fly and welter weights, and eight ounces from middle to heavy.

HANDS They must be protected, so bandage is used. Professionals are not allowed more than eighteen feet of two-inch soft bandage. They can also use one-inch zinc oxide plaster tape, but no more than nine feet unless they are light-heavy or heavyweights, who are permitted eleven feet. The bandage can go round the wrist, back and palm of the hands, but the knuckles must not be covered. Bandages are always put on in the dressing-room where, for minor fights, the gloves are also put on. But for championship bouts, the bandages must be rubber-stamped by the Boxing Board of Control's inspector, and the gloves fitted in the ring.

INFIGHTING Not the most spectacular way of winning a fight, but it has a vital part to play in the overall conquest. The phrase means, literally, that a boxer is getting close in to his opponent and delivering a two-fisted attack, usually on the lower part of the body. At worst, it has a weakening effect. At best, it can cause the guard to be lowered and the way opened for a blow at the head.

JAB A nasty punch, from the receiving end. It is a shorter version of the left lead, with the wrist turned as the punch lands. The extra power generated by the wrist turn is quite substantial, particularly as the blow is delivered with a straight, not bent, arm. With a little extra length, the jab becomes a hook, a favourite punch of mine which somebody kindly christened 'Enery's 'Ammer. It won me a few fights.

KIT The rules of professional boxing merely state that contestants must be stripped to the waist, box in regulation boots without heels or spikes, with regulation shorts. Plus, of course, gloves and tapes, stockings and a protector.

I was as superstitious as the next boxer. We are nearly all as bad as each other. I always boxed in royal blue and white. I had a dressing-gown of royal blue velvet with a Union Jack on it. Very smart, but I would never clean my boxing boots. I did it once as an amateur, and I was the only boxer in the team to be beaten. Never again, though I always did put in new laces . . . another superstition. White nylon football socks completed the outfit, except for the protector. I don't keep many boxing items, but that particular protector is an exception. Naturally convex, it had served me for thirteen years before an Italian heavyweight hit it three times in the same fight and changed the shape to concave!

LEANING A fighter is not supposed to lean on an opponent, but when a fighter is taking a pummelling in the stomach, there is not much else he can do. He doesn't get any marks for being clever, but the rest helps, especially if the lean becomes part of a clinch from which the referee rescues him with a shout of 'break'.

MUSCLES Tremendously important to the boxer, not only in the arms but in the stomach as well. Medicine ball exercises develop the tummy muscles; roadwork does likewise for those in the legs; and sessions on the heavy punchbag take care of the arms. But muscles are not the be-all and end-all of a good punch. Correct timing is almost as important, though without the power there will never be any glory.

NEUTRAL CORNER One of the two corners not occupied by the boxers. Between rounds, the referee will be found there totting up his marks. During rounds, it is the place where the boxer still on his feet goes after knocking down his opponent. He stays in the neutral corner, hoping the opponent isn't going to get up, but on his toes, ready to be told by the referee to 'box on' if the opponent does rise to his feet.

OPEN GLOVE Fighting with an open glove instead of a fist will bring a rebuke from the referee. He has to see the crime first, of course. When I've been gouged by a thumb, that has been on the blind side of the referee, too. But unless the glove is opened with deliberate intent, the sound of the slap is the give-away.

POINTS They are awarded for effort, i.e. going forward, and for accuracy and frequency of punch. The best way to score points is to go in there first. He who hangs about usually gets hurt. The British system is to give a maximum of ten points for each round, with the scoring being done solely by the referee who will probably find only one point's difference between the two fighters. In the United States, they award a maximum of twenty points each round, with the scoring being done by judges at the ringside, and the referee having a casting vote only when necessary.

QUENCH Boxers might appear to take a swig, but they don't. All that water, taken between rounds to quench their thirst, is squirted out of their mouths. They swallow not a drop. The stomach must be kept empty. Why? Imagine what would happen to any liquid in a stomach hit by a thundering punch. Uncomfortable is a mild description.

ROUNDS In amateur boxing there are only three rounds, and they last three minutes each. In professional boxing, fighters between eighteen and nineteen years of age may not box for more than an aggregate of twenty-four minutes, and those between nineteen and twenty box for no more than thirty minutes. Each round lasts three minutes by general custom, but there is provision (though not very often taken up) for rounds of two minutes in contests of ten rounds and less. The interval between each round is a minute. Title fights are of fifteen rounds' duration. Others are mutually agreed, and are usually of twelve, ten, eight or six rounds.

SECONDS Ten of them measured on a stop-watch can be the difference between victory and defeat. So can the white-clad gentlemen who leap into the ring between rounds. To the uninitiated, it may look a mad scramble, but the operation is organised down to the last piece of cotton wool. There are only sixty seconds in which to work, and the best of seconds have decided, before the end of the round, what they have to do for their man. By the time they reach him, bottle tops are already unscrewed, the ice-packs are ready, and so are the cotton swabs and the mixture of adrenalin and Vaseline for stopping bleeding. There is a lot to get through in less than a minute.

TACTICS Not easy. Whoever it was who coined the phrase about the boxing ring being the loneliest place in sport knew what he was talking about. Professional boxers go into a fight with some knowledge of their opponents, but on the night most or all of the preconceived ideas can easily get turned inside out.

I always started a fight slowly. I knew what I could do, but I was never too sure about the other fellow. My manager, the late Jim Wicks, was one of the shrewdest characters in boxing. But he always used to say: 'Be careful. Just feel him out in the first round.' After that, when Jim and my seconds had had a little more time to have a look at how a fight was going, we might start changing things. Tactics are all right up to a point, but if the other fellow's reach is six inches more than yours, the only advice is to keep out of his way, and nip in when you can.

UPPERCUT For some reason this is the glamour punch, the one the kids all talk about and want to use. These days it does not finish as many fights as it did. Defensive strategy has become more scientific. Nevertheless, a perfectly executed uppercut can shorten a fight. Delivered with either hand, it starts from around the top of the shorts, comes all the way up, and explodes – ideally on the chin. But it is almost as damaging driven into the heart or the solar plexus.

VERSATILITY Nobody reaches the top in boxing without being able to mount a varied attack. The man who has only one specialist punch will not go very far. He will find that an experienced opponent will quickly work out the danger and do something about it. To be able to attack on all fronts and defend from all angles is the difference between the boxer who is going somewhere and the one who isn't.

WEIGHT The golden rule is never to take into the ring more weight than is necessary. If a boxer is carrying more than his natural poundage – and I have known boxers let extra weight develop in the hope that they will be able to punch harder – his speed and timing may go. This is not such a problem in the lower divisions, where most non-title fights are taken at a pound or two over the official limits. But the big men, like me, have to discover their best fighting weight. Mine was 13 st 7½ lbs. Early in my career I went in at 13 st 9 lbs, and 13 st 10 lbs. A couple of pounds might not seem much, but at the lower weight I could move more sharply and I still had the weight there for punching. There is no secret about how a boxer keeps his best weight. He cuts out a lot of the starch from his diet and does plenty of roadwork.

X – THE COUNT OF TEN Any boxer who has received the perfect punch is not going to beat the count. As one who was knocked out four times, I know what I'm talking about – and none of those k.o.'s hurt a bit. The best way of beating the count is to wait as long as possible, and here the almost universal introduction of the mandatory count of eight, for humanitarian reasons, has given many a boxer the chance to clear his head. In my fighting time, I saw misguided characters leap off the canvas too soon and stick their chins into another packet of trouble. It was not until the Queensberry Rules were drawn up in the 1860s that the 'out of time' count was settled at ten seconds. Under Broughton's Rules of the 1740s, boxers were allowed half a minute to resume fighting, and in the London Prize Ring Rules of 1838 the figure was set at a mystifying thirty-eight seconds. I assume they were still packing horseshoes in their gloves!

YOUTH In theory, boxing is a young man's game, or should be if he is a good boxer. Yet I wasn't the only old 'un that carried on to within two months of his thirty-seventh birthday. Archie Moore, the former world light-heavyweight champion, was still boxing past his fiftieth birthday. There is no compensation for experience, and certainly the heavy men have an advantage in that their fights are usually fought at a slower pace than the bantams and feathers. The little men have to get a move on, and can be virtually worn out by their early thirties. All boxers have only so many fights in them. I lasted so long because I paced myself. But my idea of the best kind of fight to see is an up and coming youngster with some potential up against a wily old pro who is possibly starting to go down the other side. Usually, youth triumphs, but learns a lot on the way.

ZEST Without it, no boxer has ever won anything. I used to look for it in an opponent's eyes. Then watch them come off their stool at the start of another round. As soon as the spark disappeared, as soon as they came out with more of their weight on their heels than their toes, I knew I was on my way. I had spotted the give-away signs.

ROUND 4

Punching for Pay

Turning professional is a momentous decision. If it is the right one, there can be riches at the end of the rainbow. If it is the wrong one, there can be only a few poor pay-days before the fighter discovers that he has made a big mistake. None of the professional promoters wants his services, and there is no way back to the carefree amateur days. The Amateur Boxing Association rules are very strict. Once a boxer has decided to go, he has gone, and there is no way back. A golfer or a professional footballer, can have his amateur status restored – but not a boxer.

The motive for turning pro, for most of us, is the possibility of augmenting one's income. At the outset, the youngster accepts that he is going to have to continue with his normal job, and train and fight in his spare time. It can't be otherwise. There are not enough promotions to keep hundreds of boxers in full employment, and even if there were I wouldn't want to go back to the days when the average boxer was having a fight every month.

Just occasionally, I have wondered whether I would have become a professional if I hadn't twice won the ABA light-heavyweight title and achieved Olympic status. But not for long. Olympic man or not, what swayed the decision was that if we won a fight, George or me, we would be able to contribute around £40 into the family kitty. Forty quid, in 1954, was about four times as much as we were picking up as plasterers, even with the odd boost of overtime. Thanks to our strict boxing education, first at the Bellingham club and later at Eltham, the one thing we were not lacking was confidence in our ability to do well.

I suppose both George and I always knew, deep down, that boxing was eventually going to be about turning professional. Money has a loud voice when it is scarce. Dad, also christened Henry, was one of the unlucky ones who fought through two world wars. He never picked up more than a tenner a week in his whole working life, and at the time when he might have been showing me and George, and brother Bernard, what this growing up business is all about, he spent three and a half years in Burma proving to the Japs that a bloke weaned and raised in London's Elephant and Castle area can survive in the trees, even without Tarzan and Jane. But with Mum bringing up three hefty boys to whom the demolition of food, the tearing of clothes and the scuffing of shoes was a way of life at the time a pound note had to last two days, can you wonder why George and I had a shrewd and healthy appreciation for that forty-pound carrot?

While money was certainly the most influential factor in deciding the way our boxing careers would go, there was also the question of pride. And the magnetism of the ring. George and I wanted to know just how good we were. As amateurs we had found a level. But after the Olympics, there was nowhere else for me to go. Either I hung around for four years waiting for the 1956 Olympics in Melbourne, or I contributed my whack towards Mum and Dad having an easier time.

I've heard all sorts of reasons for fighters making their minds up to punch for pay, but money, believe me, is far and away the most common. And why not?

When the talented amateur goes legitimate, and stops cashing in on his silver cake-stands and the tankards that are incongruously rained on chaps who are supposedly spending their social hours going as easy as possible on the ale, he applies to one of the British Boxing Board of Control's area committees for a licence. The cost, even in these days of raging inflation, is no more than the price of spending an hour in one of the West End's more plush establishments.

Tommy Farr goes after Joe Louis during their 1937 world heavyweight title fight.

Thirty-six years on, Tommy and Joe talk it through again without distracting their wives Martha and Monty (*right*). Do Tommy and Joe bear the marks of our tough trade?

How a boxer's hands are taped. Jim Watt prepares for a training session.

Opposite
Working on the speed-ball, my old pal 'Nosher' Powell, a great favourite with London fight fans.

Using the gymnasium mirror to check that he is getting it all right is former world lightweight champion Jim Watt.

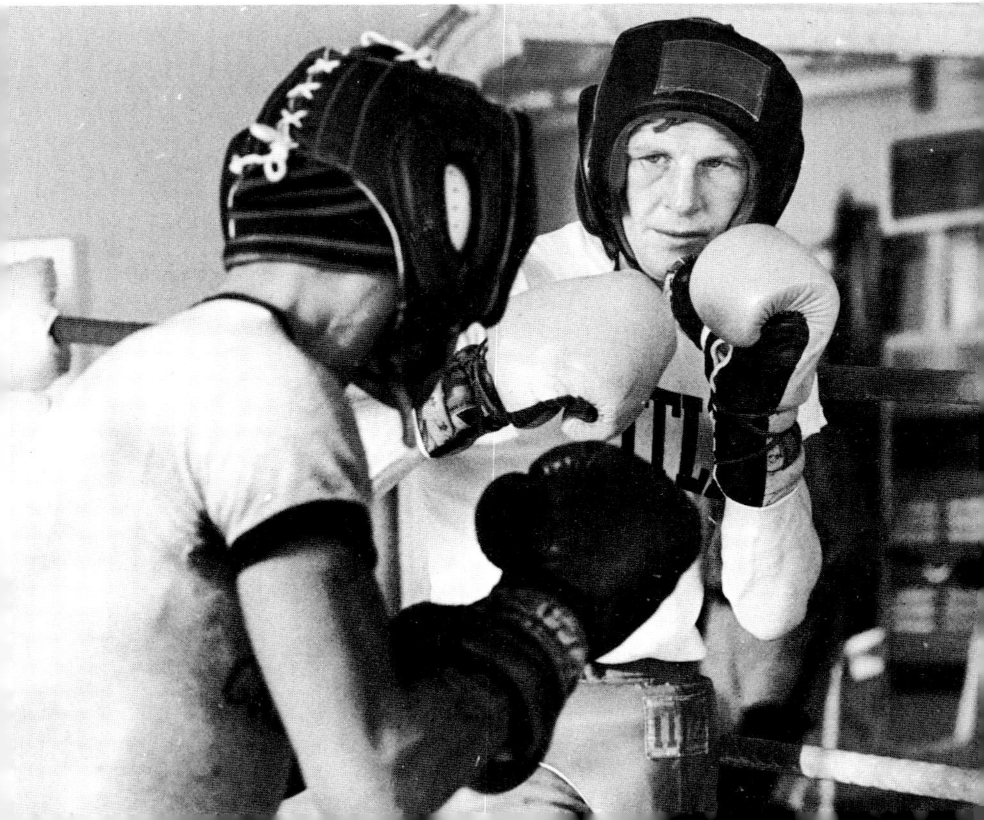

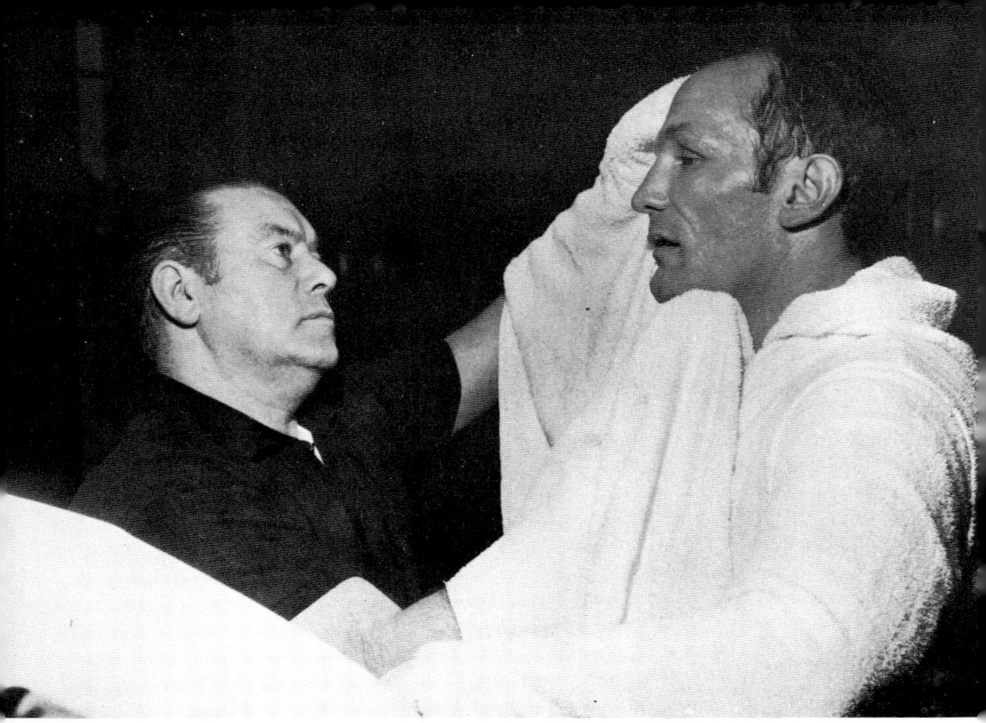

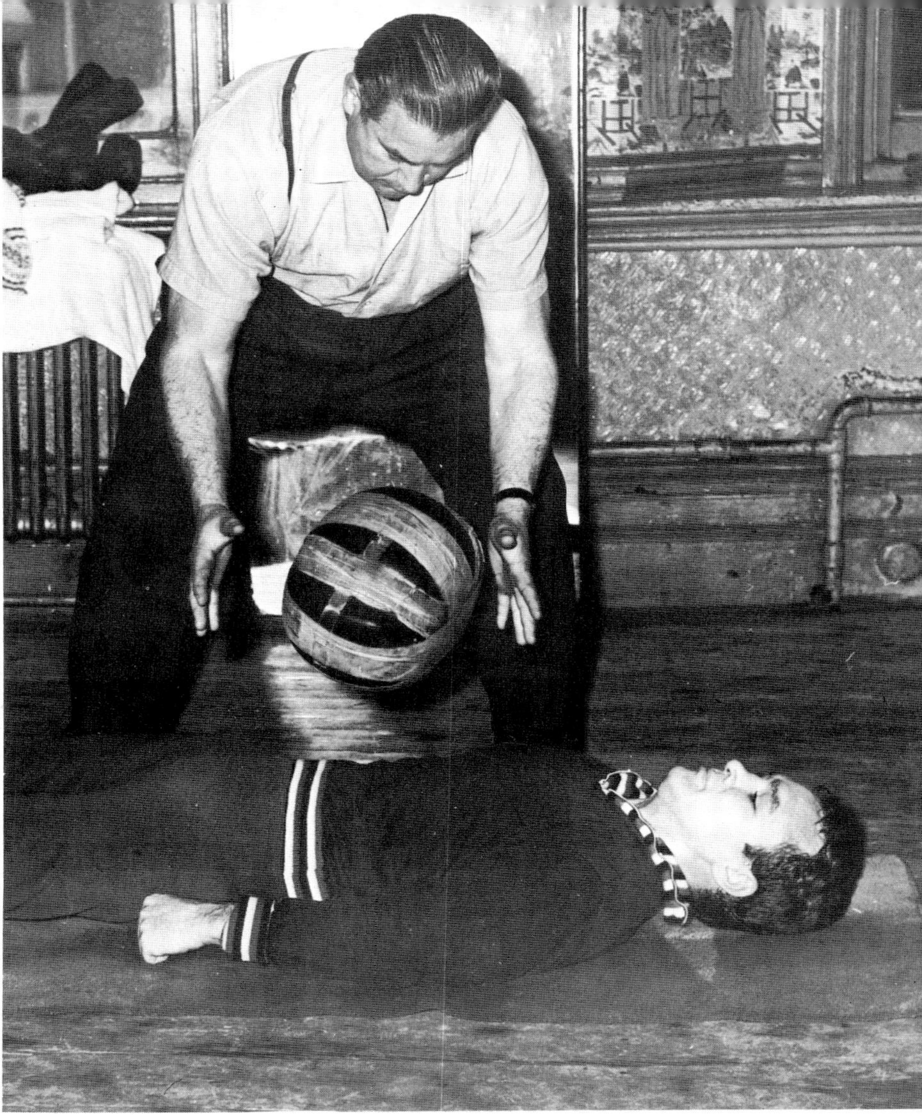

One way of developing tummy muscles. Trainer Danny Holland drops the medicine ball on Dave Charnley's stomach. It's no worse than a punch. . . .

Opposite
Above: With Danny Holland, the finest cuts man in the business, after a training session at the Thomas A'Beckett.

Below Manager Jim Wicks with me and my twin brother George, who fought as Jim Cooper.

Opposite
Floyd Patterson, the former world heavyweight champion, is greeted by singer Salena Jones after a training session. A publicity picture, yes, but the sweat pouring down Floyd, even over Salena's left hand, indicates how hard boxers have to punish themselves during training.

Howard Winstone demonstrates one of the ways a boxer can build up his muscles.

Kevin Finnegan, the former European middleweight champion, is a ballet enthusiast, and also quite a talented painter. He used to practise with members of the Royal Ballet, and it all helps co-ordination and timing.

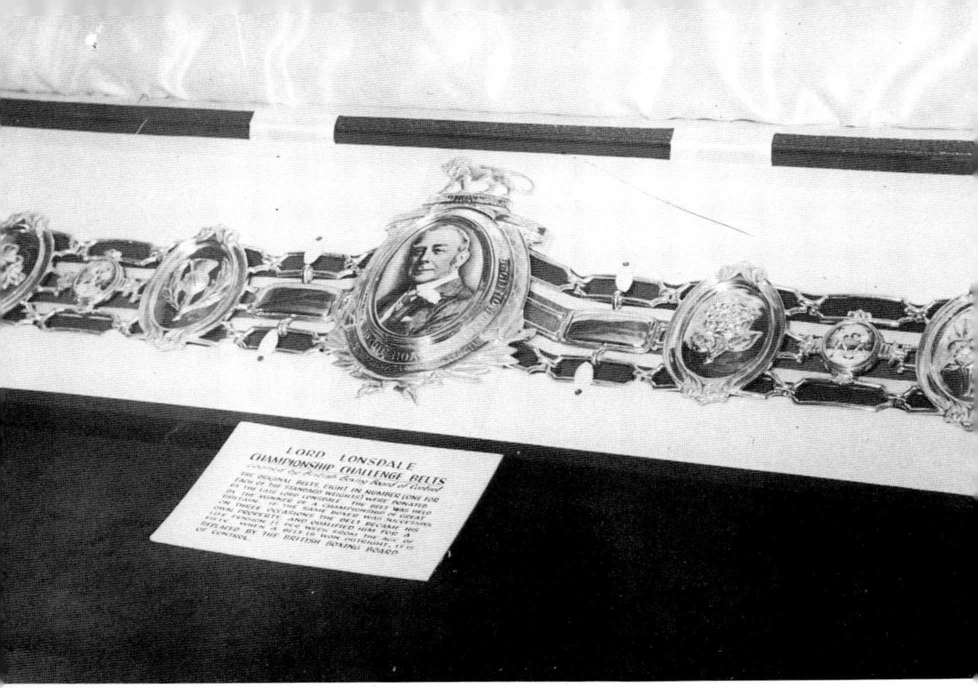

The Lonsdale Belt, awarded to British boxers who win three title fights.

Jack Broughton (*left*), the 'father' of boxing, depicted during his bout with George Stevenson.

The application, however, is the easy part. The granting of it is entirely, and rightly, a different matter. The standards applied by the British Boxing Board of Control are among the most severe in the world. I would put the proportion of successful applications at no more than one in twenty.

The first hurdle that the prospective professional has to clear is the medical, and this provides more casualties than all the gloves in the game put together. Nobody makes the decision to join the paid ranks but the boxer himself. I would distrust the motives of the manager who coerced any lad into becoming a professional. In fact, two of the best, the late Jim Wicks who looked after my affairs, and Terry Lawless, who produced a stable of world champions including John H. Stracey, Maurice Hope, Jim Watt and Cornelius Boza Edwards in the late seventies and early eighties, let the boxers come to them. Of course, Jim and Terry had concern for money. Managing boxers is a business. Nevertheless, with them, the welfare of the boys counted above all else.

Jim Wicks, a shrewd South Londoner whose origins were in the dockland area of Bermondsey, was like a second father to me. Until he died, well into his eighties, we met frequently for lunch, a carry-over from our fighting days when we used to have a meal at a different London restaurant every week.

George and I were boxing for Eltham and waiting to go in the Army when we first went to see Jim. If money had been his first consideration, he could have slapped the contracts on his dining-room table and got us to sign them there and then. We would have done, too. Not that we were that green, but it was a whole new world to us, and we would have done what we were told. What we were told by Jim was to delay becoming professionals until we had come out of the Army.

So we got Jim's first piece of advice for free, and good advice it was, too. The Army, like all the Services, were dead keen on boxing. But if we had gone in as professionals, we wouldn't have been allowed to box for them and so we wouldn't have been given any special treatment. Had we turned professional, Jim would have been able to arrange a few fights from which he could have taken his percentage. But he didn't.

Jim reasoned that the Army would take us all over the place, and give us time for training. He was quite right, but he might have been cutting his own financial throat because George and I did quite well in the Army. We got known, and the tapping started. We were offered all sorts of inducements to sign as professionals for this or that Tom, Dick or Harry. But we'd taken to Jim. He hadn't tried to take us for a ride, so one of the first rides George and I took when we came out of the khaki was on a red London Transport double-decker from Bellingham to Jim's home a few miles away at Eltham.

We told him we were ready to sign, and would have done so there and then. But Jim was a great publicist. Twins turning professional together was different. So Jim contacted the BBC and suggested that the signing ceremony should take place on one of their sports programmes. It did. We all got carried away to the extent that George and I even boxed a round for added effect. It ended when the makeshift ring collapsed – the one thing that wasn't fixed. The publicity value was immense. The whole of Britain's sporting world knew that the Cooper boys had joined the paid ranks.

Nowadays, it is slightly different. The medical standards for the novice boxer are higher. First of all, the prospective professional must let the boxing authorities know the name of the doctor who is doing the medical. Usually, it is either the lad's general practitioner or a doctor attached to the Boxing Board, but obviously he must be acceptable to the Board.

The first snag is that the lad pays the fee. It can be hefty because the form the doctor has to fill in comprises a daunting four printed pages. That document probes not only the boxer's health but that of his father, mother, brothers and sisters.

Respiration, the central nervous system, heart and limbs –

they all come under the closest scrutiny. The Boxing Board have added another one since I went through all that. It is a skull X-ray for which, again, the applicant must pay. I regret that that test wasn't compulsory in my time. It would have been nice to be able to prove that I had got something between my ears. But, seriously, before any man embarks on a professional career, he will have been proved constitutionally perfect by most of the devices known to medical science. So is our youngster now clear to leap into the ring and battle for booty?

Not likely! It's that cash business again. It puts temptation in front of an awful lot of blokes who have only the faintest idea of what the game is all about. It's all right if our boy has a good amateur reputation. That constitutes a track record which is well exposed, and his level of performance is known. He has already proved that he has the reflex action and the natural ability to take care of himself in the ring.

It is the unproven applicants who worry the men who run boxing. It is too easy, particularly in times of recent recession, for a hefty male who had won something of a street-corner reputation for being able to look after himself, to see boxing as the means to a better end. This type has to be protected from himself. The good name of boxing has to be protected, too, and so a private trial is arranged at a gymnasium. This will be watched by members of the Boxing Board, and they won't be looking so much at his aptitude for dishing out punishment as at his ability to avoid taking it. Only when this test has been satisfactorily undergone is a licence issued, and with it comes a warning that it can be revoked at any time.

Until the late sixties it was possible to become a professional at the age of only sixteen. I agree with those who believed it was too young and subsequently raised the age limit to eighteen. It was thought that this would help the amateurs raise their standards, but in the light of experience and demand, boxing's age of consent has been reduced to seventeen. I know that several pre-war boxers like Len

Harvey, who won the championships of Britain and the Empire at middle, light-heavy and heavy, fought for money *before* they left school. But that was back in the fight-to-eat days.

If he hasn't already done so, now is the time when the young boxer needs to think about getting himself a manager. Fighters sometimes do try to go it alone, but I don't see how it can ever be entirely successful.

Scotsman Ken Buchanan, who held the world lightweight title from 1970 until 1972, looked after his own affairs. But he never seemed to be able to sell himself to the public. Even his four world championship fights were all in the United States. I don't think that Ken, a classy former ABA featherweight king, made the money out of the game that his exceptional talents deserved, and in the late seventies he was tempted to make a come-back.

Under George Francis's managership, John Conteh became world light-heavyweight champion when he beat Jorge Ahumada, from Argentina, in 1974. Subsequently the Liverpudlian decided to manage himself, and lost not only the world title – it was taken away from him because of the difficulty of getting him into the ring to defend it – but a small fortune as well.

With Jim Wicks, I never had to worry about anything but the training and the fighting. Everything else was Jim's department. He got me the best terms and, of course, opponents that were good for me. No manager worth his percentage is ever going to let his man take a fight in which he hasn't at least a seventy-five per cent chance of winning. If the odds are that bad, you don't take the fight.

There is no way that a youngster just coming into the game can know the potential danger of prospective opposition. I learned this fact of life in my first professional fight, arranged by Jim Wicks. I fought a chap named Harry Painter, whose more successful boxing days were behind him. I clouted him twice, and it was all over, in the first round. That gave me a tremendous start, and with Jim's shrewd guidance I ran up a sequence of nine wins before my first defeat.

To be quite honest, there was never any thought of defeat in my early fights, and that is the way it should be when a young fighter is trying to build a reputation. The progress of the apprentice professional is carefully monitored. Until he is eighteen, he is severely restricted in the length of the contests he takes, and their number. First, he is limited to four rounds of two minutes, and there must be at least twelve days between contests. Any variation can be made only at the discretion of the Boxing Board of Control.

After eighteen, providing the Board decide that he has made sufficient progress, the youngster can graduate to a six-rounder of two minutes each round, and then on to six rounds of three minutes each. Beyond that, the eight-, ten- and twelve-round fights await - and, hopefully, the fifteen-round title fights.

But, between turning professional and the title fights that have to be every boxer's ambition, there is a long, hard road along which the best companion is a sense of dedication. No youngster should be under any misapprehension. When he decides to punch for pay, it isn't the easy life he is choosing. For a start, the last thing he does is turn his own job in, and one of the first is to arrange training a couple of nights a week and, probably, on a Sunday morning as well. That, of course, is just to keep in trim. When the next fight is coming up, training is intensified.

What George and I did, when we joined Jim Wicks, was to use the famous gymnasium over the Thomas A'Beckett pub in London's Old Kent Road. That place must have produced more champions than any other gym, and when we went there it was presided over by Danny Holland, Jim's trainer.

Danny looks back over half a century in boxing, is acknowledged as the finest cuts man in the world, and even in his seventies was in constant demand as a corner man.

At the start of our careers, George and I were so keen to

get our hands on some of the shekels that we would train most days. We were working then for a plastering contractor named Reg Reynolds who ran his own business. He would even arrange the shift duties so that we could get off early and chug up to the Thomas A'Beckett in our almost clapped-out eight-horsepower tin can on wheels.

Then we would go through all the usual routine of sparring, shadow-boxing, skipping, punch-bag, speed-ball, the lot. We'd give it about a couple of hours, and leading the good life was no real problem. We were too tired to fall off the rails. We lived at home, and with a Mum like ours, there were no problems. Our diet was mostly a simple steak and salad. It seems expensive, I know, but I've always taken the view that buying good food and eating well is one of the ways a boxer invests in his own future. Later, as the fights became more important, I took to leaving home to train, for three weeks in the middle of my career, and for five weeks in the later stages when the old body took longer to lick into shape. As I said, the words boxing and luxury should never be used in the same sentence.

Away from home, the routine is readily established. Fighter, manager, trainer, sometimes a chief sparring partner ... that's all. If too many people are employed the situation not only gets complicated, but costly. Specialised sparring partners can live elsewhere and just report to the gym.

So when I went away for a spell of the monastic life, Jim came with me, Danny Holland – and brother George. That was all. We were fairly typical. You can't vary the preparation all that much. You grit your teeth and enjoy it. Or pretend to. When the alarm goes off at around quarter to four in the morning, you tell yourself that it is going to do you good and you just get on with it.

By four o'clock, we'd be on the road, Danny or George on the bike and me buried inside a track suit and the heaviest boots I could find. It might have been a throw-back to my

Army days, but I never did find any boots that stood up better than a pair of solid squarebashers.

The amount of roadwork varies from boxer to boxer. Four or five miles was enough for me. I used to watch my fitness closely. I was always, even between fights, relatively fit. I only wanted to harden off and to acquire the stamina to go fifteen rounds. I've seen too many boxers 'over-cook' themselves in training. By the time they get into the ring, they've left their wind and half their wisdom on the road. I mean that. Any boxer who climbs into the ring *not* feeling one hundred per cent fit, is going to find his concentration going, and that is the kiss of death.

When I went in against Joe Bygraves for my first title fight, I knew within the first minute that I was too heavy. We'd done it deliberately, but we'd made a mistake that I never repeated.

I was worried more about myself than I was about Joe. That's why he nailed me in the ninth. I just hadn't the breath left to recover. As you go through life you learn something from every circumstance, and that was one of the most important, and painful, lessons I ever had. So the roadwork was severely regulated until I had it just right, and that was four to five miles.

Mind you, I did it non-stop, so it was normally around three-quarters of an hour. I never liked it. The boxer who says he is enjoying his roadwork is a bloke I'd like on my side in a liar dice school. It doesn't get easier as the fight date draws nearer. Oh no. The trainer is being paid to make the boxer fit, so every time they go out, the trainer is lowering the target time for the run. Or, if the weight is not coming off quickly enough, he is adding an extra sweater or two. Danny Holland and I never fell out over training runs. But there were times when I could cheerfully have put one of my Army boots through the spokes of his bike.

Back at base, usually a hotel in the country, most of the clothes would have to be peeled off. The object of the exercise was, after all, to raise a sweat. For ten minutes or so after a run, if the boxer has been giving it all he's got (which he should do, otherwise he has been cheating himself), he continues to sweat. Then it's into the bath and back into bed. That does for most boxers, but before I went to sleep again, I liked a rub with spirit to close the pores.

I would wake up about half-past eight, have a light breakfast, read the papers and then go for a walk before lunch-time.

I do mean lunch-time and not lunch. As the fight draws nearer, the boxer gives up eating and drinking for pleasure. He takes aboard the minimum amount of food he needs, and reduces the liquid intake accordingly. I must admit that I've always been glad that I was a natural heavyweight. Some of the lads who are closer to the scales than they are to their wives, go through torture trying to keep just inside their vital fighting weight.

So, early afternoon, it is off to the gym. The number of rounds a boxer spars depends on how close is the date of the fight. It is all a question of regulating the build-up. For big fights, the manager will try to hire a sparring partner who has something of the style of the opposing fighter and, believe me, this is one area of preparation where it is foolish to economise.

When I first fought Cassius Clay (as he then was) – the 1963 ten-rounder at Wembley and not the world title fight at Highbury three years later – we imported from America a fighter named Alonzo Johnson. He'd been on the unlucky end of a close points verdict when he fought Clay in Clay's home town of Louisville, and having sparred with Clay, could imitate his style almost to perfection. Not agreeing with the Louisville verdict, Alonzo was more than ready to help us. As that was the fight in which I put Clay on the canvas, and the one-minute interval between rounds was stretched by the time it took to effect running repairs to Clay's torn glove, I reckon Alonzo earned his corn – which was £1,000 plus his keep and his fare.

After an hour or so in the gym, we would go back to the hotel for the main meal of the day, eaten in mid-afternoon. Every boxer has his own preference. Mine, as I've said, was for steak and salad. But we all have this in common; we do cut down drastically, or cut out altogether, the sweet things and the carbohydrates like bread and potatoes. I liked my evenings to be relaxed. Television or a game of cards, or perhaps listening to Jim Wicks tell a few stories about the old days of boxing. But after a phone call home, it was always bed at 9.30. The alarm was due to go off just before four a.m.

I have often been asked why boxers do their roadwork at such an unearthly hour. There seems to be a hint of mystery about it, as if there is some magic that only rubs off at dawn. Well, there isn't. Boxers go out at that time of the morning simply because there are fewer people about, and the roads are not full of petrol fumes. Try taking a couple of walks, one at four a.m. and the other twelve hours later. The difference is remarkable. In three-quarters of an hour on the road, I reckon I used to take in a fair quota of oxygen. Mixing it with carbon monoxide would not have done me much good.

That self-discipline might even have been one of the principal causes why, even ten years after quitting the ring, I felt nearly as fit as I was when I was fighting. I can take thirty-six holes of golf a day in my stride, literally. There are more bonuses to boxing than just the money.

Money, the stuff we're all in the game for, becomes a problem when a boxer is at the top of the tree. Times haven't changed, and our crowd-pullers are still fighting just as much for the tax man as themselves. I sometimes wonder how much my contributions to the Exchequer influenced my being made a member of the Order of the British Empire!

Seriously, there was one year in the early sixties when I earned around £36,000. In those days a quid was probably worth five times what it is now. Out of that £36,000, the taxman helped himself to £29,000. In five years between 1960 and 1964, I fought only eleven times, and it surely doesn't take a financial expert to figure out why.

I met James Hunt, the former world motor racing champion driver, not long before he finished with the game. At the time, he was taking a bit of stick. He had conquered the world and was finding it that much harder to work up the old ambition. The momentum was being maintained, but the foot wasn't being applied to the accelerator with quite the same zip. James had also discovered that there were other things in life apart from the one obsession that had driven him so hard for a number of years. I wasn't surprised that his attitude had changed slightly when he told me that for something like a hundred hours a year he was putting his life on the line for sixpence an hour. That was when James was being taxed nineteen shillings and sixpence in the pound – which means, for the benefit of my younger readers, that he was keeping just two and a half pence out of every quid he earned.

One day something will be done, surely, about sportsmen's earnings. They will have to be spread over several years. Authors, playwrights and show-biz people are able to do it, so why not sportsmen? Nobody expects an author to write a best-seller every year. In fact most authors don't even write one in a lifetime. So what is wrong with sportsmen being given the same treatment?

It is not easy. Footballers and cricketers, for instance, have the benefit of a regular income, from an annual salary paid weekly or monthly. Mostly, their earnings come from one major source, the club. But injury can wreck their careers at any time.

Golfers don't have the same risk. Neither do tennis players. But even they have peak periods in their careers when, for only a few brief years, their earnings are at their maximum.

Flat-racing jockeys are more predictable, but the risk factor in steeplechasing takes jump jockeys near the category of boxers and racing drivers.

Jim Wicks and I, when we were fighting, spent a lot of time campaigning about this issue. We once got it included in a Private Member's bill in the House of Commons, but there was never time for it to be brought up.

There is, unfortunately, no boxers' trade union. I can't see how there could be. It is a selfish game, and it has to be. There is no way one fighter and his manager are going to stop trying to get £5,000 out of a promoter simply because the same promoter paid only £4,000 for his previous top-of-the-bill.

One piece of advice I would always give to any youngster breaking into boxing is never to undersell himself. You hardly need telephones in boxing. The grapevine does it so much quicker. Whatever purse has been negotiated for a boy, he can bet most of boxing will know what it is inside a week. So, if he has boxed for promoter X for £1,000, he isn't going to prise £2,000 out of promoter Z unless there are dramatic circumstances. Jim Wicks and I were always hard negotiators. The promoters want to spend as little as they can. That's understandable. That's business. We wanted as much as we could get. That was our business. But once the bargain was settled, we observed one golden rule. We gave it all we'd got. We reckoned we owed it to the punters.

It pays a boy to get a following. Fans, given reasonable distances, will travel to see him fight. That way, the lad helps to sell tickets. That way he will be high on any promoter's list. That way, if he climbs to the top rung of the ladder, his manager will be able to negotiate terms based on a percentage of the gate.

It is important that a boxer looks after his money. It is hard-earned. I don't somehow think that I will ever receive a letter from the Inland Revenue saying that because I gave them between eighty and ninety per cent of my income in my best years, I need only pay between ten and twenty per cent in my worst years.

One of the best investments a lad can make is to obtain sound financial advice. I learned the hard way, the expensive way. It cost me a few grand, and it taught me never to make the same mistake twice. The mistake was to go into something I know nothing about.

The money was coming in nicely from boxing. Not a fortune, but enough to spare to put some into a business. There was a greengrocer's shop going at Wembley, not too far away from where I was living, so I went into a partnership. It didn't work because I didn't know enough about business nor enough about greengrocery. When it reached the stage where I had to make the decision whether to neglect my training or neglect the shop, it had to go.

Now Jim Watt, the man who won the world lightweight title for Glasgow and defended it more times than any other Scotsman has defended a world crown, got it right. He had already begun to develop a car sales and garage business in Glasgow before he made the decision to join manager Terry Lawless's world champion stable. It doesn't need spelling out how much Jim's income from six world title bouts helped the business.

I am sure that Jim, like most of us who opted to punch for pay, has few regrets.

ROUND 5

Promoters and Match-Makers

Boxing promoters have a lot in common with bookmakers. Their holiday postcards can carry a Bahamas postmark; their cigar bills, diverted, would make a considerable contribution towards alleviating the National Debt; and they spend a lifetime trying to convince the rest of us that the worry of it all just isn't worth the return.

The reason you never meet an unsuccessful bookmaker is that he doesn't stay in business long enough. The same can be said for the boxing promoter. Most of them, big, brash characters with the personality to sell themselves as well as the fights they stage, will undoubtedly argue that they are the most important men in the sport. Begging their pardon, now that I don't have to ask them for fights, I would always award that particular palm to the lads who risk getting hurt. If it is true that without promoters there would be no fighters, it is equally true that without fighters there would be nothing for promoters to promote.

Would I ever become a promoter? No, no, no! Even if I were certain of making money, I can think of many less painful ways. Like opening a pork butcher's shop in London's Golders Green on Fridays only. I sometimes wonder why the two promoters for whom I fought most of my ring battles, first Jack Solomons and then Harry Levene, didn't do just that. It would have been an easier, if less eventful life. But I never had any complaints against Jack or Harry. They staged their shows with flair and style, and that is what any boxer wants from his promoter.

Like boxers, promoters go into the game to make money. In doing so, they also risk money. Some can be operating on behalf of a syndicate, some use their own cash. But, just as nobody forces boxers to box, nobody forces promoters to promote. Like boxers, they do it despite all the hassle and aggravation, because they love the fight game. Nearly all promoters started by throwing leather, but they had the sense to quit as soon as the realisation dawned that they were never going to reach the top.

Their psychiatrists will have since told them that that was when they should have shaken the resin from the soles of their feet and concentrated their energies on cleaning windows for a living or discovering a new oilfield in the North Sea. But boxing is like a drug. You cannot kick the habit. I can't, even now. Unless I have another engagement, I am usually at the ringside on big fight nights. The BBC pay me as a member of their radio commentating team, and the cash puts the odd gallon or two into one of the thirstiest petrol tanks in London. The thrill and atmosphere of the ringside pulls just as powerfully as ever.

It is the same feeling of anticipation and excitement that makes it all worthwhile for the promoter, whether the climax is a fanfare of title fight trumpets or a small-hall show that is one of the occasions of the year for the local community. Nevertheless, invisible worry beads were invented for boxing promoters.

First, he must be licensed by the Boxing Board of Control. Although the cost of that scrap of paper is minimal, the prospective promoter must lay his financial standing right on the line. The interrogation is not quite as severe as for bankruptcy, or so I believe, but the Control Board stewards have to dig deep in order to protect the boxers and all the other officials involved. Imagine a boxer taking a tousing for a few rounds and then waking up to discover that the promoter hasn't the money to pay him.

Once his licence has been granted, the promoter's next

moves are to fix up venues and bills. The big boys, like Harry Levene and Mike Barrett, who promote on a lavish scale, will book their Wembleys and their Royal Albert Halls well in advance, probably more than a year, and put the bill together nearer the time.

Smaller promoters, taking a chance by breaking new ground, will negotiate with local councils and hire assembly rooms or public baths. It is here that the unsuspecting can take their first punch on the chin. The local authority will ask for the building to be insured for the night, for half a million pounds in some cases. Well, just as at any public gathering, things can get out of hand . . . the place could burn down. By now, the promoter will have received the message. All he does, before he starts selling tickets, is pay out.

Having booked his venue, the promoter has to think about the bill. If he is big, he will probably hand the job over to a match-maker. If he is small, he will do it all himself.

Without any doubt, the most influential match-maker in Britain in the last quarter of a century has been Micky Duff, who generally puts the bills together for Harry Levene and Mike Barrett. In fighting terms, Micky was a professional featherweight in the late forties. In match-making terms, he is a heavyweight in the world sense. Even in the United States, where promoters make a career of calling their own shots, they listen to Duff, who has also been a manager and promoter, trainer and second. The cost of his international travel each year assures him of VIP treatment at practically every airport in the world.

In the big stadia most top-of-the-bill fights make themselves. A title fight is obviously determined by the ruling body, whether it be at world, European or national level. An international contest, like the times I took on one of the leading Americans, would usually be arranged by the promoter, who would then ask the match-maker to do the rest of the bill. Harry Levene always preferred to work this way.

He would ring up Jim Wicks, tell him he had a stadium

going spare on such and such a date, and ask if we were interested in taking a fight. Our answer usually depended on how we were fixed with the tax-man. Assuming we said yes, Harry would suggest a number of opponents for us, which Jim would agree on or not. Managers like Jim could be a promoter's nightmare, but it was good for me.

I remember when we were to fight Alex Miteff, the Argentine heavyweight, for Harry Levene in October 1958. It had all been nicely sewn up when we received a transatlantic phone call to tell us that Miteff had damaged his leg in a fight and would have to pull out of our date.

That sort of thing is an occupational hazard for promoters, and Harry had already been on to contacts in the United States and knew he could get a replacement in Sonny Liston, who was threatening the rest of the world but hadn't yet become champion. But Jim had had his cards well marked about Sonny and wasn't having any part of it. Eventually, after running up a phone bill as high as St Paul's Cathedral, Harry managed to do a deal with Zora Folley, then ranked third in the world.

It turned out well for all of us except Folley, whose world ranking took a knock when I outpointed him.

That programme cost Harry a bomb in time and trouble, but the victory sold tickets for the next few Cooper fights, to our benefit as well as Harry's. Sometimes, the promoter's clouds have a cheque-book lining.

Sometimes they don't. One of the great myths was exploded by at least two optimists who thought Muhammad Ali was the passport to instant riches. How could you lose money staging an Ali fight? Easy. Ali was just about the tightest choker of all time - choke, in boxing vernacular, being the pressure a fighter, or his manager, puts on a promoter to extract the largest sum of purse money he can.

When I fought Ali for the world title at the Arsenal football ground in May 1966, we all did well - me, Harry Levene who promoted the fight, and Ali, who has put his share of the cake at $448,186. Three months later, Ali was back in town, at Earl's Court, giving Brian London, from whom I took the British heavyweight championship, his crack at the world crown. Heavily involved in this promotion was one of Britain's leading show business tycoons, but it certainly wasn't a case of sitting back and watching the money pile up. Ali's take this time was a modest $290,411, or only about three-fifths of what he grossed for fighting me. Yet the Earl's Court promotion was around £70,000 in the red by the time they had done all the sums. London was knocked out, too – in the third round.

Six years on, when Ali was working his way back towards regaining the title stripped from him while he was refusing to join the United States army and fight in Vietnam, a wealthy Irish lady involved herself in a syndicate to bring 'The Greatest' to Dublin. Ali's opponent, an unranked Al 'Blue' Lewis, was knocked out in the eleventh round. Ali choked for $200,000 – modest by his standards, but more than enough to burn the fingers of the syndicate who, to the best of my knowledge, left boxing well alone after that.

The biggest one-off loss of all was six million dollars. That is the sum President Mobuto and the government of Zaïre lost when Ali regained his world crown by knocking out George Foreman in the eighth round in Kinshasa in 1974. That was a promotional exercise to put on the map the new state of Zaïre. A postponement of two months following Foreman's cutting an eye in training didn't help, but Ali took away $5,450,000. Not bad for a challenger.

Back to the bread-and-butter boxing. Six days before the event the promoter, who by now is plaiting his fingers and hoping that nothing happens to upset his bill, must send details of all the financial aspects of it to the Control Board. He must name all his fighters, all his officials, and disclose how much he is paying them. If, by any chance, he has managed to interest television in his show, the Board will want a percentage.

Meanwhile, the promoter has been seeing to the advertising, the publicity, taking on casual staff to cope with the demand for tickets and generally battling with increasing attacks of insomnia. But, if he is a shrewd promoter, he has solved some of his problems by looking after certain boxers who are reliable performers and proven ticket-sellers.

Boxing can never be philanthropic. Life is easier for the promoter if he deals with particular managers for his middle and lower-down-the-bill bouts. He may get four boxers from the one stable. The dream of any promoter is to spot a promising youngster and to watch him climb up the bill, winning friends and fans on the way. If the lad ever matures into a title challenger, and eventually champion, it doesn't take a genius to guess which promoter is going to be able to do the business.

Mind you, when Jim Wicks and I reached the position where we were able to do our share of the dictating, we were always careful to keep an involvement with a promoter strictly on a business level.

Jack Solomons and Harry Levene bought most of my sweat, Solomons in the early stages and Levene later. We didn't fall out with Solomons, who was the top promoter in British boxing when we started. It was just that Levene got bigger and bigger, and Jack preferred to concentrate on the World Sporting Club at Grosvenor House, a venture with which, since Jack's death, I am also involved. But the promoting is done by my old friend Paddy Byrne.

Jim Wicks never thought it a good idea for me to get too tied up with one promoter. We always reckoned, even when I was only half-way along the road to recognition, that once it got around that we were too close to one, other promoters might stop coming in for us. In fact, we used to gee up Jack and Harry (who didn't speak to each other for years after an argument during a fish deal which was the last transaction they ever did together), dropping hints that we were thinking about doing this and thinking about taking that. It is a hard business, boxing. You're only in the driving seat as long as you can keep winning.

Promoters have to pull strokes. They wouldn't survive otherwise. Nobody thinks the worse of anybody who might give a razor a few points for sharpness.

It is going back a few years, but there is one story that sums it all up. From where the white, shining knight is sitting, the circumstances show boxing at its worst. Me, I think the affair is typical. The saga can only be boxing at its best for the people involved at the right end, and of those who were, I think Tommy Farr, the former British heavyweight champion, is the only one who survived into the eighties.

Back in 1936, when heavyweight James J. Braddock ruled the world, the New York State Athletic Commission had a nice, tight grip on the movement of world titles. They wanted Braddock to defend his against former world champion Max Schmeling.

Mike Jacobs was then top promoter in the United States, and the man who put on most of Joe Louis's fights. He was also a Jew, and the idea of a German becoming world champion while the Nazi regime was committing anti-Jewish atrocities was one Jacobs couldn't life with. So, cold-shouldering Schmeling, he began to negotiate for Braddock to defend against Louis.

Somehow, the Jacobs plan was leaked to Sydney Hulls, one of London's top promoters, whose immediate reaction was to try and match Schmeling with Farr and label the fight for the heavyweight championship of the world. Schmeling wouldn't have disagreed. He had knocked out Louis in the twelfth round only a few weeks earlier.

The wily Jacobs, known in the trade as Yussel the Muscle, was on the bridge of his personal *Titanic*. The world title was slipping away from him unless Louis, his meal-ticket, could be manœuvred into the ring with Braddock. Across the Atlantic, Hulls, Schmeling and Farr were in the mood to fight first and argue the political toss about the title later.

So Jacobs moved. Fast. In two directions. He contacted Farr and Ted Broadribb, his manager. They were dangled a package of four fights in the United States, one of which would be for the world crown. The offer was accepted, and that was the Hulls menace disposed of.

Jacobs then went to Braddock's camp and tabled one of the most audacious boxing deals of all time. He offered Braddock ten per cent of his own share of all Joe Louis's future earnings in the ring if he would put the title at stake against Louis. Braddock might have been called the Cinderella Man, but he must have believed in fairies for the rest of his life. Louis, who knocked out Braddock in the eighth round, had thirty-six more paid fights, twenty-five of them with the world crown at stake. Some pension. Both Braddock and Jacobs lived happily ever after.

As a manipulator, Jacobs was out on his own. But all the major promoters have to be fly fellows if they are to sell their expensive shows. Jack Solomons was never stuck for an idea or two. Publicity was his middle name, and there was never anybody from the Press, television or radio who left Jack's office empty-handed or, for that matter, with an empty stomach. Mike Barrett, who owned a dock before an unquenchable enthusiasm made him devote more and more time to boxing, would be the first to admit that his style is the more subdued when compared with Solomons. Nevertheless, he got into the act when tickets for a fight involving a Canadian heavyweight were not moving as fast as they might. So Mike contacted a circus and borrowed a grizzly bear. The bear and the boxer walked down London's Shaftesbury Avenue together, and I wouldn't like to say what caused the monumental traffic jam – bear and boxer, or the posse of pressmen and cameramen who accompanied them.

The promoting game is no good to anybody who cannot do his sums. The margin between profit and loss is comparatively finely balanced. A miscalculation such as over-estimating the popular appeal of the top-of-the-bill, or having the hall only half full, and the promoter is in trouble. These days, there are far more tickets sold in advance. There is a diminishing number of traditional pay-at-the-door customers, so the promoter is not at such risk with inclement weather as he used to be.

Today's promoters are also better protected than their predecessors. For instance, if he loses money on a show, a promoter can apply to the Control Board for a reduction in the amount of tax he has to pay, and the request will be sympathetically received. The smaller the show, in terms of finance, the less tax he will pay.

There is also a clause in the boxer's contract giving the promoter the option of engaging the fighter for two bouts inside the following seven weeks. This doesn't make any difference to the big promoter who is putting on only five or six shows a year, but it does boost the earning potential of the middle and smaller promoter who is putting on shows regularly. It means that if a couple of boxers have turned on an exciting contest, the promoter can book them again for the crowd-pulling return. If this option clause wasn't in operation, there would be nothing to prevent an unscrupulous promoter 'poaching' a fight which owed something of its excitement and drama to the match-making skill of the person who put the original bill together.

Any boxer who cannot fulfil an engagement has to pay the promoter compensation. In fact, as soon as he signs the contract, the boxer is required by the Control Board to deposit a sum of money with them which is returned only when the contract has been successfully completed.

The big promoters, who come in a few times a year, will probably spend at a ratio of ten to make fourteen. Given a title fight to top their bill, or a couple of international contests, they will probably spend something like £100,000 putting the bill together. If they have done that, then they will price their seats to gross up to something in the region of £140,000, working on the basis that they will not have a complete sell-out.

Television is only icing on the cake, because sixty per cent of fees from the media go to the boxers concerned and the Control Board. But the Control Board do put part of their share into a fund for the assistance of promoters.

The promoter has to pay the fees of a doctor, referees, timekeepers and one second for each corner, all appointed by the Control Board. He also has to provide an announcer, dressing-room attendants and the whip, the official who ensures that the boxers are ready to go into the ring on time. These are appointments of the promoter's choice.

The big promoter does not normally make boxing a full-time career. He usually has several other business interests. But the middle and small promoters ... those lads have to give it the complete go, and work to a much finer margin than ten to fourteen. Down the scale, there is not so much money about. 'Some you win, some you lose on' is a philosophy that might have been created specially for the promoter whose pockets are not quite so deep.

Typical of them is Paddy Byrne, an amiable Irishman who operates from his home in Brighton where the phone never stops ringing and the next show, in the season, is always the proverbial day after tomorrow.

Paddy, as I explained earlier, is the promoter at the World Sporting Club, London, where I am involved as Chief Executive of Sport. He does nine shows a year for us, in addition to the annual jockeys' boxing championships. He also promotes at Manor Place, Elephant and Castle, Lewisham and Walthamstow in London, plus regular commitments at Belfast, Hove and Morecambe. Throw in various one-offs at other venues, and Paddy is staging about thirty shows a year. Between September and April, he is promoting at the rate of almost a show a week.

To suggest that boxing is a full-time occupation for Paddy, and people like him, is an understatement. It is a way of life.

Paddy is the first to admit that if somebody in boxing is making a fortune, then it isn't him. But that is the way it has been for more than thirty years. Paddy is typical of the promoter who keeps the game alive by sowing the harvest others reap.

It isn't all telephone and tribulation for Paddy. Occasionally, he flies off to places like Spain and Zimbabwe. But never on holiday. Always on boxing business.

Paddy's story began with a few amateur fights, then fewer still as a professional before the Army claimed him for seven years. That little dust-up sorted out, he wandered into Jack Solomons' gym in London's Great Windmill Street in the late forties – and hasn't had a day's peace since!

Paddy is an all-rounder. At his level of operations, the budget doesn't run to specialists. He books his halls, mostly on annual agreements. He does his own match-making, organises his fighters and then gets weaving on all the rest. He has a share of an office at the Grosvenor House Hotel for his World Sporting Club activities, has the share of another in London by courtesy of Lonsdale Sports, who supply most of the equipment to our leading boxers – including me in my fighting days – and then there is his paper-swamped home in Brighton. He answers the phone, too, telling me that if he has to be the dogsbody on the day of his fights, he might as well make the role a permanency.

Paddy works within his own cash limits. He has never yet had to ask the Control Board to bale him out, and is proud of it. At his level of promoting, everybody mucks in. His timekeeper might cadge a lift with one of the boxers. Paddy always has a mate who will give a bed to save a hotel bill. Yet his bill for boxing gloves is the same as the big boys, because rules and regulations prevent the same pair being used more than once on any one bill.

Paddy keeps himself ahead of the field by attention to detail. His life is full of problems that the fans never hear about. He can't delegate because his staff is himself. Then he argues that the punter isn't interested in the promoter's ulcers. The punter has paid for his half-dozen fights, and he's got to have them. Paddy is always telling me that the glamour wore off years ago ... that he could live off his phone bills. He says that routine would get him down. I know boxers, like my old stable-mates, Joe Lucy and Teddy Haynes, who have taken pubs after retiring from the ring. Paddy Byrne gave up pubs to concentrate on promoting boxing.

Contrast Byrne's operations with those of Don King, the Black Muslim American negro who made himself a multi-millionaire promoting Muhammad Ali's biggest fights in the 1970s. Any man who can make Ali money and still hang on to some of it himself is entitled to be called a genius, and in the terms of international boxing finance manipulation, King was certainly unique. Contracts were so speckled with noughts that anybody who didn't understand boxing might have been forgiven for thinking a calculator had severed a circuit.

King exploited the potential of world-wide television to the full. He put up the idea of the Ali–Foreman fight to President Mobuto of Zaire. Be sure that King, unlike Zaire, wasn't on the losing side. King's greatest personal triumph was that morning of 1 October 1975 in Manila, where Ali had his third bloodbath with Joe Frazier. Ali won it in the fourteenth round when he forced Frazier to retire. But the real winner was King. The statistics are mind-boggling. There were 28,000 at the ringside, but the television audience numbered 700,000,000 in sixty-eight countries.

They tell legends about the old promoters like Jacobs, Tex Rickard, the man behind Jack Dempsey, and Jim Norris, who helped lift Rocky Marciano to glory. But those facts of King dwarf all the legends.

The face of boxing at the grass roots has changed considerably over the last twenty years. Many of the traditional small-hall venues have gone. Some promoters have been priced out of business by rising costs and the shortage of boxers. But in a lot of cases, when leases on buildings have run out, the property has simply been sold for other purposes.

So now we have another kind of promotion, the dinner club. The conception is a throw-back to the days of the old National Sporting Club, where the belted earls and their aristocratic friends would dine, and where the blood at the table and on the plates was of an infinitely finer quality than that spilt in the ring.

The old National Sporting Club was born in London's Covent Garden in 1891 and represented the best in boxing quality until the middle twenties. It lost some of its stature then for the same reason that I would never fight at any of the early dinner shows. I couldn't afford it, and neither could the top-liners of the twenties who could earn much bigger purses elsewhere. It is sad, but it is all about space, and space is seen by any profit-seeking promoter in simple terms of how many seats can be squeezed into it.

The promoter, in these circumstances, is the club. Or the club appoints an expert, like the World Sporting Club which has Paddy Byrne, to do that job and the match-making for them. The members' annual subscription pays for the boxing, and they can invite guests in accordance with club rules. In all other respects, the club deals with the Control Board and boxers' managers in the same way, and with the same responsibilities, as a commercial promoter.

These are the places where a young boxer can make a reputation, and the wise promoter will keep an eye on what is happening at the knife and fork venues. Eating to live, you might say. But that is a rare occurrence. In boxing people live mostly off the promoter.

ROUND 6

Managers

Boxing managers do not come cheap. Yet of all the fighters who have tried to go it alone in comparatively recent times, I can think of only one, Ken Buchanan, who became a world champion. And even Ken, who, somewhat surprisingly, learned our bruising trade in the cultured atmosphere of Edinburgh, found it impossible to reject the come-back call when it came dressed with financial bait.

I was never tempted to make a return to the ring. I didn't need the money that badly, and I have never regretted one of my earliest decisions – which was to concentrate on the fighting and leave the rest of my career in the hands of the specialists.

With all respect to Ken, and to John Conteh, whose decision to look after himself was, in its effect on his career, akin to pressing a self-destruction button, most fighters are only as good as their back-up team. For most of my career I had Jim Wicks as manager, Danny Holland as trainer, and twin George as a second. At the time I retired in 1971, I had been fortunate to earn more money out of the game than any other British boxer. I was more than happy to be the means by which Jim, Danny and George earned a quid or two as well, because we were a team who were good for each other.

To the uninitiated, the manager is the cigar-smoking and whisky-drinking fellow who takes twenty-five per cent for doing next to nothing, apart from making a few phone calls to sell his man to the highest bidder. The trainer is somewhere in the background, breaking into a sweat only on fight night. The second is the white-sweatered character who humps a bucket of water and a sponge from the dressing-room to the ringside.

If you believe that, you'll believe anything. The manager is the most important person in a boxer's professional life. More important even than the promoter who pays him. Because if the manager isn't doing his job properly, the boxer's career has little chance of getting off the ground.

What the novice boxer wants most at the start of his career is guidance, advice and experience. If he has any sense, he goes out and buys all three. They can come in one package, as long as it is labelled: Good Manager. Bad managers can destroy good boxers by pushing them too soon and being greedy for every penny, whereas even average boxers can become moderately successful – financially, I mean – if they are handled by a good manager. The most important ropes in boxing are not those that make the ring. They are the ropes that a shrewd manager has spent a lifetime learning.

Most managers are shrewd. But it is almost impossible for them to be unscrupulous. There are rules and regulations which load the dice against them. For example, managers cannot take more than ten per cent of an apprentice boxer's money. The cut rises to twenty-five per cent only when a boxer reaches senior status at the age of eighteen – and he cannot even become an apprentice until he reaches the age of seventeen.

Not much opportunity for exploitation there. Then there is the length of the contract between manager and boxer. It can run for a maximum of three years. So if the boxer thinks he has been having a raw deal, he can find himself another manager.

In my case, the glove was on the other fist. I only signed one contract with Jim Wicks. It didn't occur to me to sign another. I never realised the three years were up. After that we just went on. Mutual trust. So much so that if Jim had ever told me that he had had enough, that he was going to get out of the game, then I would have retired. I could never have had the same relationship with another manager.

There is one exception to the three-year rule, and that is when a boxer has become a champion during the period of the contract. The manager is entitled to something for having taken his man to a title, and has the option of renewing the contract for a similar period. That is fair enough, surely. I won my first titles, the British and Empire crowns, in 1959. That means that Jim Wicks and I worked together for the next twelve years with nothing legal to prevent us walking out on each other.

When I first joined Jim he had quite a stable. By the time I stopped boxing I was his only boxer, and when I said that I had had enough, Jim retired too. But for years afterwards, until he died in 1980, he still looked after my business affairs.

There was no way I needed protection from Jim, but the Boxing Board of Control lays down another important safeguard for boxers. Nobody is allowed to become a manager until he has spent at least a year in the boxing game in some other capacity, usually as a trainer, a second or a matchmaker. This means there is no danger of a boxer's affairs being handled by somebody not fully conversant with the sport.

Once I became established, my purses were split, more or less, the same way every time. The first ten per cent paid for training expenses. Then the manager's twenty-five per cent went. There is no standing rule regarding the sum of money paid to a trainer. It is a matter for negotiation, but more often than not the trainer picks up something in the region of ten per cent. That leaves around fifty-five per cent for the lad who takes the punches ... before the Income Tax man comes around. So those £10,000 purses suddenly become very much slimmer.

So what does a manager do for his twenty-five per cent? For a start, he puts himself about a bit. He never misses a boxing tournament in his own vicinity. The obvious reason for this is the boxing grapevine. He must know what is going on: what promoters are looking for on their future bills; how those boxers are coming on who might be prospective opponents for his own lads; who is negotiating for this, and why so and so took that. He may not be seen to be wheeling and dealing, but he is. And, if he is a wise manager, he will know which opponents to keep his own boy away from.

As I have said, he will play one promoter against the other in order to get the best terms he can. If he has a big stable of boxers he will either run his own gymnasium, as Terry Lawless does at the Royal Oak in London's Canning Town, or else hire facilities, as Jim Wicks did, at the famous Thomas A'Beckett in London's musically immortalised Old Kent Road.

Some managers have the touch of Svengali. Joe Jacobs, the American Jew who looked after the affairs of Max Schmeling whenever the German fought in the United States in the thirties, was one of them. It was Jacobs who climbed into the ring and persuaded the referee that Schmeling had been hit by a low blow when the German collapsed to the canvas in the fourth round of a fight with Jack Sharkey for the world heavyweight championship. That was the only time the title has changed hands on a foul.

It was Jacobs who achieved one of the most impressive feats of boxing managership when he got Tony Galento into the ring as challenger for Joe Louis's world title. Galento, whose most memorable contribution to the world of letters was the phrase: 'I'll murder the bum', stood 5 ft 9 ins but weighed nearly seventeen stone. He also trained on beer and hamburgers, a combination that, coupled with a left hook, put Louis down for a count. But in the fourth round Jacobs and the handlers were having to achieve the impressive feat of hauling 'Two-Ton' Tony off the canvas and on to his stool.

A boxer's relationship with his manager can develop into a lifelong friendship, or, as in the case with Jim and me, he can become almost one of the family. But the start must always be on a business basis. I would never recommend a relative running a boxer's life, though there have been successful exceptions.

Alan Minter, who brought the world middleweight title back to Britain in 1980, was managed by his father-in-law, Doug Bidwell. Nobody can argue against a world championship, which Alan won by outpointing Vito Antuofermo in Las Vegas - and you have to be good to snatch a points verdict in the United States - but Doug had trained Alan in his amateur days and had known him all his boxing life.

Another exception was Jack Petersen who, in just over a year of turning professional in the early thirties, had won both light-heavyweight and heavyweight British titles. He was managed by his father, Pa Petersen. I've never heard anybody use the old boy's christian name, but he had one endearing habit. Around about the middle of a fight, particularly if Jack, who never weighed as much as thirteen stone in his fighting career, wasn't doing too well, the old boy would cascade a bottle of champagne over his son's head. Jim Wicks might have delighted in taking on the bookies, but he was never that extravagant ... and I don't like the stuff anyway.

Enduring relationships can and frequently do develop between manager and boxer. The prime example in British boxing in the late seventies and early eighties has been Terry Lawless, who stands, statistically, unchallenged at the top of the British managerial boxing heap. No other British manager has guided three world champions.

John H. Stracey became the world's top welterweight in 1975, and was followed by Maurice Hope in the light-middleweight division in 1979, and lightweight Jim Watt in 1980. Jim Watt who, like me, does radio commentaries for the BBC on big-fight nights, was thinking of chucking in the game at the ripe old age of twenty-seven. He had parted company with his previous manager, Jim Murray, and Jim Watt's idea was simply to boss himself for a couple more money-making fights and then call it a day to concentrate on his garage business. Then came the momentous phone call from Terry Lawless that changed Watt's life. With Lawless, he not only became world champion but defended the title successfully three times before losing it to Alexis Arguello, the Nicaraguan who won world titles at three different weights.

Jim has told me how, when he left his native Glasgow to prepare for his London fights and world contests, he would stay with Terry Lawless and his wife Sylvie as one of the family. And the story goes, which Jim confirms, that Terry didn't want to take a cut of the Watt purse for the first five fights, on the basis that he didn't think the money he had been able to negotiate for Jim was as much as the boxer deserved.

Come the day of the fight, the manager is usually in the corner as chief adviser. That's how it was with Jim Wicks, and Terry Lawless likes to play it the same way. But the manager has a lot to do before the first bell.

There is the weigh-in to attend, and the kit to prepare. Weigh-ins are normally at lunch-time, and the manager has to take with him a copy of the contract for the fight, which may be inspected by an official of the Boxing Board of Control; his boxer's licence; and a couple of pairs of shorts to ensure that the colours of the respective boxers do not clash. That regulation is in the book to assist the referee, but it seems to me that these days it is more important that two boxers of a similar coloured skin can be distinguished easily on a black-and-white television set.

The weigh-in satisfactorily concluded, the manager must make sure that his boxer spends the afternoon resting, or if his man comes from one of the lighter divisions and has had to starve to make the weight, he may have to supervise a meal for him. In the meantime, the manager again checks the gear – boots, socks, dressing-gown, bandages, gum-shield and all that sort of thing.

Once at the stadium, the manager alternates his priorities

between making sure his boxer is kept as free from hassle as possible, and is not being turned over. The sort of thing that happened to me when I fought Brian London for the third time. The Boxing Board of Control suddenly changed the rules regarding the length of bandaging. When the Control Board steward brought in the bandages – this was a title fight – there was hardly enough for one hand after Danny Holland had unravelled it. When the steward said the bandage was supposed to be enough to cover two hands, Jim did a double-take.

He asked for the president of the Control Board, and then the secretary. Playing politics, not a crime in boxing, they sent word that they were not in control that night. But the fight had been sold to radio, and was timed to go out at 9.30. So Jim, having more than a shrewd idea just how much aggravation would be caused if there was no action for the air waves, dug in his heels and told Harry Levene, the promoter, that unless the president and the secretary sorted it out, Messrs Cooper and Wicks would be sitting in the dressing-room at 9.30.

We won. The president himself doled out another three yards. But it was hardly enough. The fight went the distance and I finished with bumps on my hands. Yet, had it not been for Jim's persistence, I could have done myself a frightening amount of damage. My mate Brian London's head was one of the hardest in the business, in more ways than one.

After the fight, the manager has to make arrangements to collect his man's purse money, usually on the following day. Then he is required to furnish his boxer with a statement of accounts. That is when fighters, especially if they have lost, tend to wonder whether it was worth it.

Managers also have moral obligations, which mostly fall into two areas: taking fights and weight-watching. As a heavyweight, I didn't have to watch my weight, other than trying to achieve what I regarded as my ideal poundage as far

Boxing, late twenties style. The man facing the camera is the legendary Len Harvey.

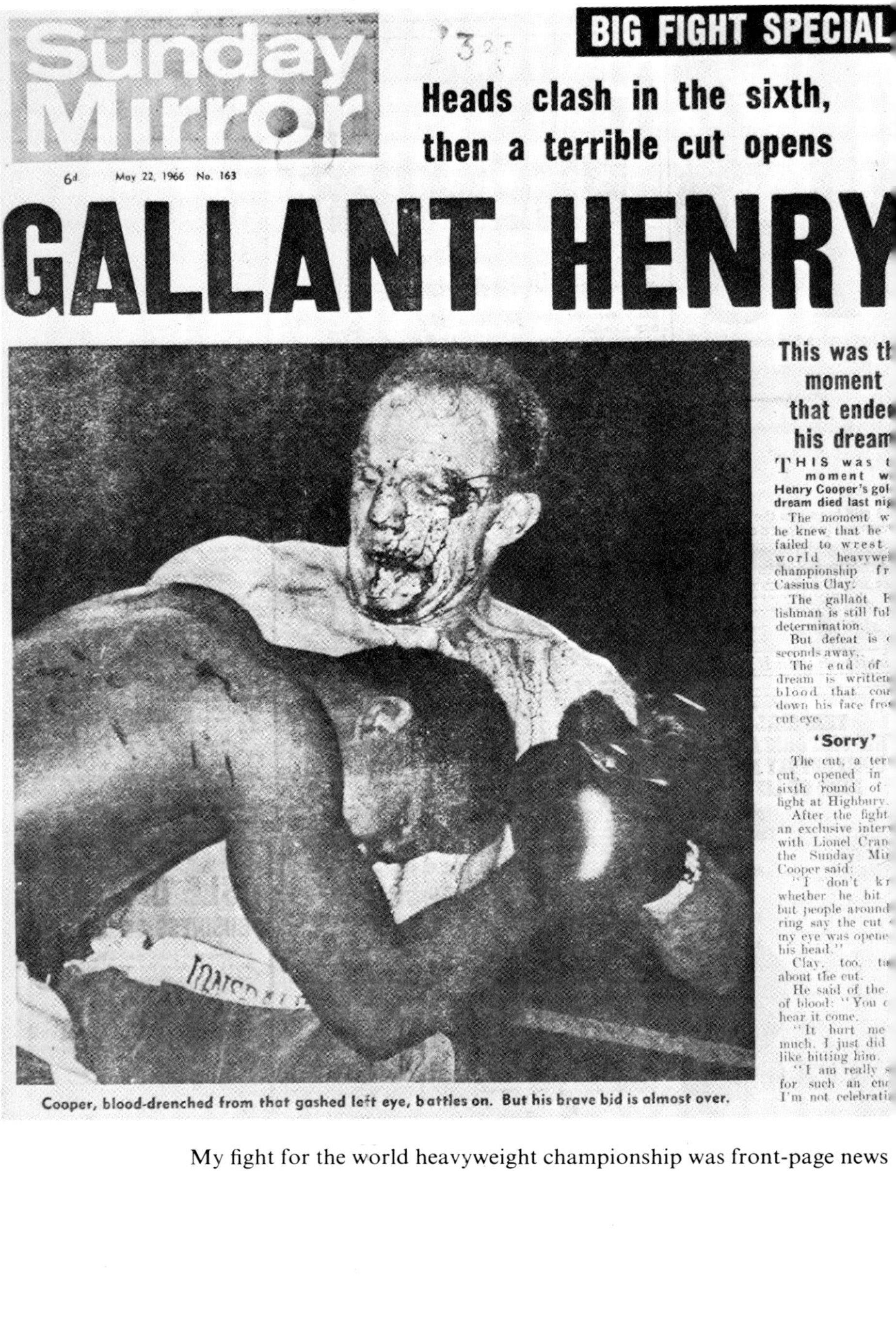

Sunday Mirror

6d. May 22, 1966 No. 163

BIG FIGHT SPECIAL

Heads clash in the sixth, then a terrible cut opens

GALLANT HENRY

Cooper, blood-drenched from that gashed left eye, battles on. But his brave bid is almost over.

**This was th
moment
that ende
his dream**

THIS was t
moment w
**Henry Cooper's gol
dream died last nig**

The moment w
he knew that he
failed to wrest
world heavywe
championship fr
Cassius Clay.

The gallant E
lishman is still ful
determination.

But defeat is
seconds away.

The end of
dream is writte
blood that cou
down his face fro
cut eye.

'Sorry'

The cut, a ter
cut, opened in
sixth round of
fight at Highbury.

After the fight
an exclusive inter
with Lionel Cran
the Sunday Mi
Cooper said:

"I don't kn
whether he hit
but people around
ring say the cut
my eye was opene
his head."

Clay, too, ta
about the cut.

He said of the
of blood: "You c
hear it come.

"It hurt me
much. I just did
like hitting him.

"I am really s
for such an enc
I'm not celebrati

My fight for the world heavyweight championship was front-page news

Sunday Mirror

Telephone: FLEet-street 0246
Sunday, May 22, 1966

The dramatic ending

PICTURES ITV AND BBC COULDN'T SHOW

moment of the cut eye—and the beginning of the end for Henry.

Referee George Smith takes a close look and says: "Box on."

A gallant Cooper goes back on the attack against Clay but defeat is staring him in the face.

It's all over . . . outstretched arms signal that Henry's attempt has failed.

'WHAT A WAY TO FINISH'

HENRY COOPER'S exclusive talk to LIONEL CRANE

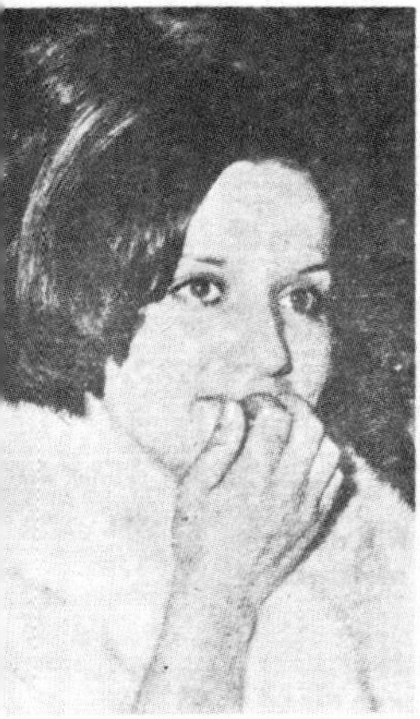

ension outside the ring . . . Henry's wife Albina watches, and soon the tears will fall.

STRAIGHT from the ring, Henry Cooper came to tell me exclusively about the tragic end to his fight with Cassius Clay.

A blood-stained towel covered his head, and when he lifted it I saw that the cut over his left eye was at least one and a half inches long, and terribly deep.

Henry said: "What a way to finish! I don't know whether he hit me, but people round the ring say the cut over my eye was opened by his head. I don't know."

Lefts

He went on: "I was catching him with my left hand well.

"I got him with some good ones. They were straight lefts. I didn't get a hook on him—not a real one.

"He was fighting better than the last time. He wasn't clowning around.

"He kept holding me. It was like a vice. I couldn't get away. In the sixth round, when the eye went, I knew it was a bad one. I couldn't see.

That was why I went after him But it was no good."

Jim Wicks, Henry's manager, interrupted to say: "If the ref hadn't stopped it I would have."

Henry went on: "I was forcing it right from the start. I was after him all the time.

Jab

I felt good. Up to the finish there was no trouble with the eye not even a nick.

Perhaps I was trying a bit too hard. But I wanted to get after him. He was good, fast and clever but his left jabs were not hurting me. They were not all that powerful.

"I thought things were going well. Then BOMP! Well, what can you do? It's no good worrying."

As he lay stretched full length on the massage table in his dressing room with his brother George and his personal team round him, I asked him the big question: Was this the end of his career?

Still game, he said: "I can't say. I can't say. I want to give up fighting. Albina (his wife) wants me to give up. So does Jim Wicks.

"If I'd won, if I'd become world champion — yes, maybe I would have quit. I always wanted to finish at the top.

"Even if that had happened, me and Jim would still have thought about it carefully. It would have had to be something fabulous to make me fight again, two hundred thousand pounds or something like that, and even then I would have thought about it."

Henry went on: "Now I don't know. I only need one more victory to get my third Lonsdale Belt outright, and that's tempting.

"I was ready for this fight. Everything had gone well for me.

Cut

"Jim Fletcher, the coloured boy who came over to spar with me, was great. He had me working just the way I wanted to work.

"And I've never been worried for a moment. As a matter of fact until I got to Highbury tonight I've never even thought about the fight.

"I mean, I didn't lie awake thinking if Clay does this, I'll do that. As a matter of fact, I didn't lie awake at all not one night.

"I saw Albina when I got into the ring. I know how she must be thinking but I know something else too. All the five weeks I've been away from home training I've talked to her on the phone every day.

"She always said the same thing. 'Henry, don't worry. Do your best. Win or lose, we've still got each other and that's all that really matters.'

"Poor little soul, she's gone through more than I have.

"Well, O.K. It's over now and me and Albina and the boy will go off for a holiday. A friend has offered me a house in Bermuda and I think that's where we'll go."

I was still standing beside Henry when a doctor came to examine the cut. He told Jim Wicks that it should be treated by a specialist in hospital.

He said: "This can't be patched up. It must be attended to by a surgeon or it will not heal properly."

Relaxed

What a miserable way to end a splendid day. I was with Henry from early morning and I have never seen a man more relaxed and at ease on the eve of the greatest night of his life.

From the weigh in we drove to Welling, Kent, where he has been staying. All the way down in the car, Henry was smiling and relaxed and waving cheerily to well-wishers on the streets and in other cars.

After lunch he sprawled half-dozing in an easy chair watching television and laughing at the cracks the rest of us made as we played rummy for pennies.

When we left for the fight, he behaved no differently from any other man going from the suburbs to London for a night's work.

As we drove to the arena he hummed to the tunes on the car radio. Little groups of people who had found out the route he was going to take, waved to him as he went by.

Smiled

He smiled at all of them and waved back.

We arrived at Highbury two hours before the fight and for the first hour the dressing-room was filled with friends who came to wish him well.

The words "Good luck" became a monotonous repetition but Henry, placid and in his usual quiet good humour, acknowledged them all modestly.

Only in the last twenty minutes before the fight did he show a slight edginess.

He asked his brother George to get his rosary out of his jacket pocket and lay on the table holding it in his bandaged hands.

Printed and Published by THE DAILY MIRROR NEWSPAPERS, Ltd., at Holborn Circus, London, E.C.1, at Mark-lane, Manchester, 4, and at Saffolk-road, Belfast, 11. Sunday, May 22, 1966

. . . and my own version appeared on the back.

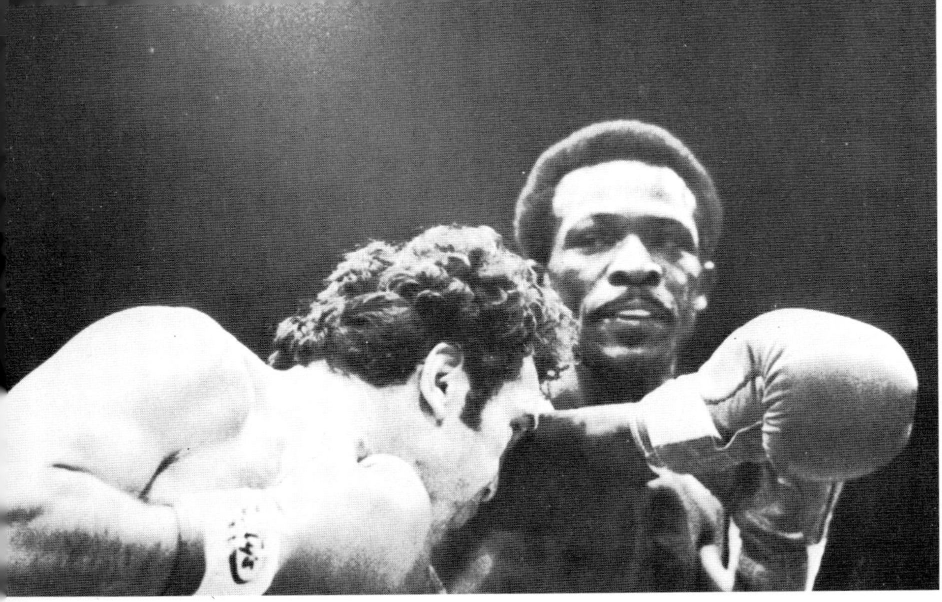

Maurice Hope, the former world light-middleweight champion, aims a right at challenger Rocky Mattioli during the successful defence of his world title.

Cornelius Boza Edwards (*right*), another of Britain's world champions, on his way to winning the super-featherweight title from Rafael 'Bazooka' Limon.

The spray flies off Joe Frazier's face as he takes a right from Muhammad Ali in their third, and last, fight in Manila, which ended with Ali keeping his world heavyweight championship.

Ageless Archie Moore (*right*), successfully defending his world light-heavyweight title against Yolande Pompey of Trinidad in 1956.

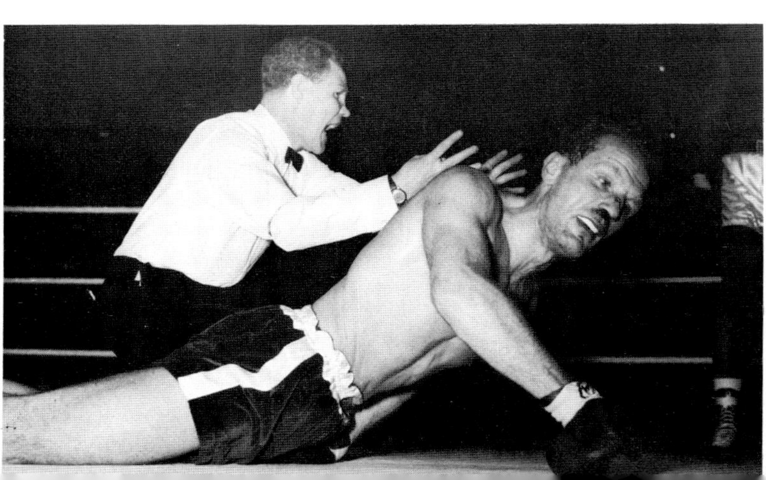

Opposite
Henry Cooper in action . . . against Billy Walker . . .

. . . Floyd Patterson . . .

. . . and Patterson again . . . though action, in this instance, is probably overstating the case. It was the best punch I ever took, and I didn't beat the count.

Randolph Turpin's greatest night – 10 July 1951. He takes a left from Sugar Ray Robinson in order to give one, but this time the shrewd Robinson is using his right arm to deflect the blow.

From an earlier vintage: Ted 'Kid' Lewis landing a right on Johnny Basham. The picture was taken in the early twenties, and the style of referees' dress has changed somewhat.

World champion. Alan Minter after he had confirmed his superiority over Vito Antuofermo in June 1980 by beating the former world champion for the second time.

'Thanks, pal, we had a good scrap.' Terry Downes (*left*) and Paul Pender after one of their world middleweight title fights.

as it affected my performance in the ring. If I was too heavy, for example, I just wasn't mobile enough.

Lower down the scale it is a crime if, just to grab the proverbial fast buck, a manager lets a young boxer stay in a weight division which he is naturally growing out of. I don't care if he is approaching title class – a lightweight who is struggling to keep below 9 st 9 lbs and is continually draining himself to make the weight, should be kicked up into the light-welterweight division, even against his own protests. The middleweight who is struggling to make 11 st 6 lbs should be told to forget about it and aim for the top of the light-heavyweights.

There is only one way to box, and that is safely. In simple terms, that means being 100 per cent fit as a minimum, and 105 per cent if possible.

Let me tell two stories to make the point. Len Harvey's was one of the most revered names in British boxing. I think he had the distinction of fighting at every weight from fly upwards. Certainly he fought for welter, middle, light-heavy and heavyweight titles. As Harvey grew heavier he went up the scale and became a champion in all such divisions except welter, even though he was never quite big enough to be a natural heavyweight. But he didn't have twenty-one title fights by starving himself into a weak condition.

When I turned professional, remember, I had been the Amateur Boxing Association's light-heavyweight champion in 1952. Two years later, at the age of twenty, I was obviously heavier. I had the good left hand and twin George had the better dig with his right.

We were both heavies, but we never wanted to fight each other. Would you fight your own brother? So I watched the calories in order that I could get down to light-heavyweight. But the good punch in the left mitt wasn't knocking them over in the gym. Shrewd Jim Wicks spotted the trouble, and we sorted it out. I stopped trying to be clever. Opponents started going down in training, and I never fought professionally at anything other than heavyweight. I can only plead that at twenty, you don't know the half of it. I might have become light-heavyweight champion. But then again, I might never have been strong enough.

The good managers will also keep a fighter away from an opponent whose style does not suit him. For instance, I never liked meeting southpaws. I had to meet them later on, because the higher you get up the ladder, the more the choice of opponent is restricted. But I nearly always found myself falling over the southpaw's leading foot. His right foot was nearly always where I wanted to put my left.

Although Sonny Liston was always on offer, before he became world champion, Jim Wicks would never take him. I didn't mind, and the same applied to several leading American heavyweights. Sonny was bad news. His sheer brute strength meant that over a lengthy fight he was likely to wear you down. If you let him slip too close, misjudgement of one massive swing could lead very quickly to an immediate invitation to do some stargazing.

One of the truest sayings in boxing is that a good big 'un will always beat a good little 'un. So there is no point in any boxer having ambitions beyond the capabilities of his physique. If he has, it is the responsibility of the manager to make him see sense.

Sugar Ray Robinson, who won the world middleweight championship a record five times in the fifties, always wanted to be king of the light-heavyweights. At his peak Sugar was rated, pound for pound, the best in the world. But when he chanced his arm by tangling with Joey Maxim, with the world cruiserweight title at stake, he took a bad beating. When the body is taking punches heavier than it is equipped to stand, the danger is obvious.

When it comes to the fight itself, most boxers prefer their manager to act as chief adviser. Usually, the manager has been through it all as a trainer. Terry Lawless, in fact, supervises all the activity at his Royal Oak gymnasium.

Lawless differs from a lot of managers. He came in the hard way, from the bottom up. His apprenticeship in boxing goes back almost the whole of his lifetime, which, professionally, has been spent entirely in London's East End. He was doing his stuff at the ringside in the mid-fifties.

Other managers, particularly in the United States, buy up promising fighters and concentrate on the business side. Joe Louis's was the classic case. When the 'Brown Bomber' decided it was time he turned professional, he asked a Detroit drug-store owner to look after him. John Roxborough took in a Julian Black as co-partner, but it was New York promoter Mike Jacobs who licked up most of the gravy, and for years after his fighting days were over Joe still owed the United States government millions of dollars in unpaid taxes.

Fortunately for the image of boxing, the Joe Louis saga is unique, though I would never deny that cool, calculating managership can make fortunes. After all, that is what we boxers pay our managers for. I know that Floyd Patterson would agree with me. Floyd, the first man in the history of boxing to recapture the world heavyweight crown after losing it - he won it first when beating Archie Moore and later regained it from Ingemar Johansson - won an Olympic gold medal at Helsinki in 1952.

He was persuaded to turn professional by Gus D'Amato, who then did an astonishing job by keeping Floyd away from all the dangerous men. He even manœuvred a title fight with Pete Rademacher, the 1956 Olympic champion. Good business? I'll say. It was Rademacher's first professional engagement! Floyd Patterson appeared in twelve world title fights, and considering that he wasn't renowned for his ability to take a punch, I reckon that was fair management.

But it was management United States-style. I prefer the British way. There is no denying that any boxer is a meal-ticket for his manager. But this side of the Atlantic, we seem to eat in a more acceptable fashion.

ROUND 7

Trainers and Seconds

There is an art in being a boxing trainer - the art of psychology. If I wanted a quick character reference on a stranger, and my life depended on it, I would send the fellow to somebody like Danny Holland or Terry Lawless. They have seen them all: the lazy and the enthusiastic; the self-propelled and those who have to be pushed; the smart and the shifty. Danny and Terry, after their long years in boxing gymnasiums, have seen them all come and go, and some of them have gone quicker than others. There are no bad apples in the successful boxing establishment, and Lawless, though a man of sentiment, knows where to draw the professional line. Even champions have left his stable.

Most boxers can train themselves, up to a point. The longer I stayed in boxing the less I needed a trainer until near the fight. I'm talking purely about the business of getting fit and staying fit, of course. But in the early stages of a boxer's career, the trainer is his best friend, or, if the lad decides to buck the system, his worst enemy. From a wise trainer, the novice boxer will learn good habits to sustain him through an entire career. Because most trainers have done it all themselves, and the best of them are so steeped in the game that, like Danny, they go on and on into their late sixties and seventies.

Danny was born, bred and has lived most of his life in the area around Bermondsey docks, on the south bank of the Thames in London, an area once prolific in amateur boxing clubs. Danny was good in the ring, but not so good at keeping his feet the day he fell down a ship's hold and fractured his skull. That stopped his fighting, and that is how boxing welcomed into its ranks one of the legendary trainers, a man so highly regarded that even in his advancing years he was still flying all over the world looking after British boxers.

For Danny, like Terry Lawless, boxing is a full-time occupation. But Danny is a trainer first, second and last. The worries of doubling up as a manager are not for him. Danny runs the Thomas A'Beckett gymnasium and is especially proud of taking Alan Minter to the world middleweight championship. I only wish I could have done the trick for Danny a few years earlier.

Most gymnasiums of any repute seem to be on licensed premises. Publicans are traditionally strong supporters of boxing. Occasionally, boxers will use sports clubs or athletic clubs, but not often. That sort of club usually has good reasons for not wanting to be involved with professional boxing – there may often be a high proportion of schoolchildren among their membership – and they are not likely to possess the specialised equipment needed by fighters. Nor is the trainer likely to be boss of his own show, and that is vital.

A visitor to the Lawless establishment is immediately aware of how important that is. Terry can have a dozen or so of his stable at various stages round the training circuit, and he is aware of what each of them is doing. He is conducting an orchestra, with eyes in the back of his head.

Terry has two assistants, Frank Black and George Wiggs. They help him run the training, and there isn't one of the Lawless lads who doesn't want Frank and George in the corner he fights.

There is a full-size ring, four punch-bags, a mirror for shadow boxing, a bike and mats for body-building, muscle-developing exercises.

It suits most trainers to use their premises from lunch-time till early evening. Very few boxers being full-time, for most of them training is restricted to about three evenings each week. Work must come first, but most have arrangements that permit them to take time off when they build up for a fight.

Between fights, three-quarters of an hour at a time is probably enough. There are sessions on the punch-bags, a spell of shadow boxing, some time on the mats and a little physical training, like skipping. Just enough to keep in trim and maintain co-ordination. Each trainer knows his own boxer, and just how much of what kind of work he needs.

The nasty part of the year is when a boxer reports back to the gym at the beginning of the winter season. If the scales register bad news, a fighter can expect to be sent on the road wearing specially weighted boots. It is then that they wish they hadn't neglected their condition.

When the fight date is fixed, the trainer puts the screws on. The roadwork is stepped up, because once a boxer's legs go, in the ring, the end of the fight is in sight. In the gym the training has to be geared to the duration of the bout, which can be anything from a six-rounder to the long title slog over 15 three-minute rounds.

First, there is the loosening-up, and then the trainer has to make a decision about clothing. How much a boxer wears depends on how near he is to the weight he wants. The plan is for the boxer to reduce gradually, hit the target a couple of days or so before the bout, and then hold it.

The easiest way to do this, and to save a lot of pain and anguish in the later stages of training, is simply to watch liquid intake. Losing weight is about dehydration. But a boxer doesn't have to suffer too much if he is sensible. To get down to the 13 st 7½ lbs that was my best fighting weight, I used to start with a careful summer behind me. I'd perhaps be half a stone heavier than I wanted. I stopped drinking tea as if it was about to go out of fashion, eased off on the bread and potatoes, without cutting them out altogether, and lost the unwanted poundage steadily.

Heavyweights don't have weigh-in problems. But the other

lads do occasionally hit trouble at the scales. If it is a question of losing only a few ounces, either a visit to the toilet or a sauna in a track-suit will usually do it. If not, then a brisk skipping-rope session and a rub-down is the answer. If that is not enough, the scales are usually checked.

It may be embarrassing to the trainer concerned, but I haven't yet met a fighter who didn't delight at the sight of his opponent struggling with the scales. It gives them a one-upmanship boost just when they need it. If ever I could see a way of unsettling my opponent at the weigh-in, you bet I would take it.

Mind you, I would never go to the same extent that Muhammad Ali did. Not that I minded all that jumping and screaming – I reckoned he was doing a good job selling tickets. Occasionally, though, even Ali overdid it. There was one particular weighing-in ceremony at which one of the official doctors wanted to have Ali carted off for a *mental* examination!

I like the story Jim Watt loves to tell about Terry Lawless, then acting in his managerial capacity, which illustrates, when we are down to the nitty-gritty, what boxing is all about. That is the survival of the fittest inside the ring, and of the shrewdest outside it.

Jim was over in Madrid to meet Perico Fernandez for the European lightweight title. Jim was the champion, and Fernandez, former world light-welterweight king, was stepping down a division to nick the title for Spain and make himself a soft quid or two while he was about it.

A Press conference was called. Jim and Fernandez sat at a table with a bottle of iced water between them, and nothing was more certain than that Fernandez's stomach was in the same state as a foreigner's in the Sahara. The bottle drew his eyes like a magnet.

Terry waited a few moments, then poured a glass of water and placed it in front of Jim. Fernandez's eyes rolled again, and again. Then Jim picked up the glass and poured the whole lot straight down his throat. With typical British politeness, Terry refilled the glass and stuck it in front of Fernandez, who didn't dare touch it and left the conference convinced that Jim had no weight problems. Certainly he had fewer than Fernandez, who was outpointed.

Back to the gym. Assuming that it is a title fight for which the boxer is preparing, he will do between ten and fifteen rounds, depending on how much work the trainer thinks is needed. The fighter will always wear a headguard – postponements because of injury are expensive – and heavier gloves to prevent doing too much damage, either to his hands or to his opponent who, more often than not, is likely to be one of his stable-mates. Hands must be bandaged.

The action will always last three minutes, just as in a fight. The rest period will always be one minute. Just as in a fight. Sometimes, the trainer will change the sparring partners for specific reasons. A lighter opponent will speed up the boxer's footwork and punching. A heavier man will enable him to punch as hard as he can. In one round, the trainer may want the emphasis on punches to the head. In another, punches to the body. All the time, the trainer will be correcting minor faults with calls of: 'Elbows in . . . feet together . . .' and so on.

While all this is going on, the boxer should be absorbing one vital lesson, an asset that not even the best of trainers can teach him, and that is how to pace a fight. It comes only from experience, but unless the ability is acquired the chances of a boxer lasting fifteen rounds will always be suspect.

Some boxers never learn to pace. They don't go very far. Rarely beyond eight-rounders, and there is no big money to be made there. The novice professional is all at sea. In the amateur ranks he has fought only three rounds. He can go crash, bang, wallop. Stamina doesn't come into it, unless he gets caught by the big dig. So he learns to go six rounds.

With experience, I was able to change the pace to suit the circumstances. I learned to watch for the crisis round that all boxers have. It always comes. The timing is off, temporarily.

A bad mistake that affects the confidence, momentarily. It might arrive early in the fight, in the middle, or near the end. But I always made a point of doing something about it if it was my opponent who was having the crisis, or, if I was the one in trouble, I would try to pretend it never happened.

Some fighters are what we call winning fighters. They only look good when they get a good start. Brian London was one of those. If you didn't take him out early, he would take you all the way, he was so tough. The first time I fought him, the referee had to stop the fight in the first round. But when I took his British and Empire titles we had to go the full fifteen, and it was the same when we met again five years later. Nevertheless, the final score was: Cooper 3, London 0.

I must admit that Brian, early in his boxing days, was not my favourite fellow. I don't think I would have won a popularity award from him either. Eventually, though, we became fair old pals, and if there is a chance to have a drink together these days, we take it. By and large, boxing enmity doesn't flow beyond the ring. Big fight night seems to make too many demands on a fighter's social time, especially if he should be at or near the top of the bill. But at small-hall shows, most of the boys have a gargle and a leg-pull afterwards.

Once out of the gymnasium ring, the boxer will see which part of the area or piece of equipment is free. But not until he has towelled down and changed his sweat shirt. I used to reckon that if I hadn't punished myself in the ring, I hadn't been training properly. Many people have told me that the most fascinating sight, on their first visit to a training session, has been the sight of the shirt gradually changing colour as it darkens with sweat. Armpits first, then shoulders, and then the level descends to the stomach and back.

If the trainer has the mats free, he will indicate that the boxer does a stint there, with one of the trainer's assistants, clip-board in hand, recording the performances as his man goes through weight-lifting exercises to strengthen abdominal muscles; others to keep hips mobile, and so on. The target changes daily, at least I used to like it to. Twenty press-ups on Tuesday meant twenty-five on Wednesday.

After the mats, one or other of the punch-bags might be free. There is the heavy bag, which simulates an opponent. I could either whack it with my heavy punches, stand off it to measure distance, or close right up for a spell of in-fighting, giving it those fast combination punches to the body.

The heavy bag hangs from the ceiling. The swing-ball is attached to ceiling and floor by an elasticised rope with the ball at about average chest height. As the boxer is never quite sure of the angle at which it is going to return to him, the swing-ball is very good for sharpening reflexes. Then, usually on a platform and hinged above a boxer's head, is the speed-ball. The ball is oval, secured at one end, and if the trainer hears a sound like the throbbing of jungle drums, then he knows, without looking, that his boxer has a good rhythm going and that there is little wrong with his co-ordination.

The bags are another sure way of working up a tidy sweat and, if the wall mirror was clear, I liked to cool down with a spell of shadow boxing. Now a lot of people, the uninitiated, argue that they can't see the point of looking through a mirror because, since it is the boxer's brain that is telling the fists what punches to deliver, he knows what is going on. That, frankly, over-simplifies the effect of the mirror. In it you see how your own punches appear to your opponent. Are you disguising them well enough? Are your feet in the right place? Perhaps you are punching too much on the back foot. Is that straight left straight enough? It is surprising what faults the mirror reveals and, I need hardly say, the timings for a shadow session are precisely the same as in the ring ... three minutes at a time with a one-minute rest, and the progress entered down on the clip-board.

The gym bike is rarely idle. As I grew older, I found that regular roadwork would keep my legs in good trim. As a heavyweight, I needed stamina more than speed. But the little fellows like Charlie Magri, who need to buzz round the ring, will spend more time on the bike than I ever had to.

Charlie, who was ABA light-flyweight champion in 1974, and flyweight in 1975–76–77, won the British professional title within a few months of joining the paid ranks in 1977. He is a fitness fanatic who has to be seen to be believed. If Terry Lawless orders a session for 2.30, then Charlie, who was a tailor's cutter in London's East End, will be at it an hour earlier, and he will keep at it until he is stopped. At less than eight stone, there isn't much of Charlie. He sweats like a river in flood, and if he loses a couple of ounces that is about as much as he can.

Cycling session over, there is the skipping rope to come. As I have said, I liked this. It was this gym routine, above all others, that I used to find impressed the lady visitors - yes, boxers do get quite a few - more than most. Whether it took them back to their days at school, or whether it is the sight of husky males proving that skipping is not entirely the province of the female, I wouldn't pretend to know. But I will recommend the exercise to any weight-conscious male, with the proviso that he stops as soon as he starts becoming breathless.

In the gym, the boxer will ask for ten minutes, or a quarter of an hour if he feels up to it, and will punctuate the time with sharp bursts. The talents in an average boxing gym would make a chorus line good enough to grace any television spectacular. I must try that one for charity some time!

What I have described is the basic training routine. But trainers in the Holland and Lawless class will throw in extras, things aimed specifically at an individual, or to polish something that will be of particular use in their boy's next contest.

For instance, Danny Holland used to like bouncing a medicine ball on my stomach while I was lying on my back. It wasn't due to any misguided sense of humour, either. Only those of us lucky enough to have been hit in that area by the full force of a heavyweight's fist can have any idea how it feels.

When we fought a southpaw, we would hire southpaw sparring partners. I had to work on getting my left hook in behind an outstretched right arm. We would also ask somebody in the gym – Danny or brother George probably – to put on one of those big instructor's pads on his right hand and let me work on the problem. The pads are about the size of a man's head, and the trainer wears them like a glove. He waves the hand about to give the boxer a moving target and takes the force of the blows on his palm.

At the level at which top-class trainers usually find themselves operating, they do not have to spend much time on the basics. They expend more of their energies on polishing. Boxers who have done well at the amateur game want teaching, mostly, how to bridge the gap between amateur and professional status. But the smaller trainer, approached by the lad who sees money to be made, will have to involve himself in much more basic instruction. No doubt the lad will bring enthusiasm, but will not have much else to offer.

The novice boxer may even have to be taught to punch properly, which is with the back of the knuckles. To use any other part of the hand is to risk damage. Punching with an open glove is a waste of time and effort. Referees don't award marks for 'slapping', which youngsters frequently do when attempting to achieve the impossible feat of extending their reach.

It is important that a boxer should know when and how to go into a clinch. There is no percentage for any boxer, when he knows he is heading straight into trouble, in continuing to take more punishment. The clinch not only gives him the chance of taking a breather but, if he is able to lean a little on his opponent, shortens the range of his adversary's fists.

No boxer travels along the road to success without acquiring the ability to get 'inside' his opponent. This trick of the trade has a two-fold bonus. The opponent's body is exposed to short, rapid-fire punches that sap his stamina, and when he wants to retaliate his blows must travel round the outside of the in-fighter's elbows, obviously losing power on the way. Basic instruction is incomplete until the novice has also been taught the art of feinting, and how to use the ropes for ducking and dodging. Without all that, the inexperienced man is on a collision course for a quick headache.

So far, so good. But how can the trainer be certain of an income? When they are as well respected as, say, Danny Holland, they will receive either salary or commission for running a gym. Their reputation will attract bookings from boxers and managers. They will run the establishment, renting out the facilities of the gym by the hour, and they will always be on hand to give personal advice. That doesn't come for free, and there is no reason why it should. The trainer is in business. His services will also be hired for assisting the preparations for a big fight, and for work at the ringside itself. When I joined Jim Wicks in 1954, I think he had fourteen boxers. Danny looked after us all.

The most dangerous enemy any boxer has, apart from the other fellow's fists, is blood. His own! The trainer who is able to stop it need never be short of a job. The best exponents of this art of my time are Angelo Dundee, who looked after Muhammad Ali, Terry Lawless, and Danny Holland.

On numerous occasions Danny and Terry have saved their fighters from defeat. For this reason: referees are extremely wary of cuts, especially around the eyes. If a boxer looks bad, with an average second working on blood spurting from a cut, the referee is very unlikely to chance his arm. When Terry or Danny are in the corner, the referee reckons that they will be able to do something about the damage and, consequently, will allow another round before deciding whether to stop the bout. In those extra minutes a boxer can become a new man. Danny and Terry have done it again.

Two classic examples concern Danny. When Joe Bugner went to Las Vegas to meet Ali, he took Danny with him. The fight was still in the opening round when Bugner, suddenly, erupted in a pool of red. But instead of stopping the contest, the referee gave Danny a chance. It was all he needed. With constant patching up, Bugner lasted the full twelve rounds before losing on a points verdict.

Danny fixed me up brilliantly when I fought Dick Richardson at Porthcawl in September 1958. Dick and I were in the Army together and knew all about each other. I wouldn't describe myself as a refined fighter, but compared with Dick I was right out of the cultural top drawer. Give him a rough-house and Dick was happy. If there wasn't a rough-house, then he would create one.

Not many referees are powerful enough to disqualify a man in the first round of a fight, and Dick was a stone bonker cert to take advantage of this. Out he roared, as soon as the first bell went, and though I was expecting trouble, he still cracked me with his head, splitting the skin from the eyebrow to the middle of the forehead.

At that stage of my career I was beginning to worry about cutting so regularly. It had happened in my previous three fights. But Danny sorted it out and I came back to stop Dick in the fifth round. Cuts rarely affected my performance after that.

Speed and planning are everything in the interval between rounds. Those sixty seconds tick away quickly, and a boxer caught on the other side of the ring when the bell goes can use up the first seven or eight seconds just getting back to his stool.

Danny, in the corner, was organisation personified. He would be on his way up the steps as soon as the time-keeper's hand moved towards the bell. He would have a swab on a stick poking out of the corner of his mouth, or two if I had been badly cut. In his right palm would be a pad of gauze. He carried the bottle of adrenalin in his left hand, the back of which would be smeared with Vaseline. A mixture of the two would staunch any cut.

I doubt if many surgeons could stop bleeding as fast as the

expert boxing second, and the surgeon doesn't have the problem of doing it all again three minutes later.

Our routine never varied. My gumshield would come out first, and then Danny would go to work on the cuts. I liked the refreshing gargle from the water bottle - who wouldn't? - but I would never swallow, and neither will most fighters. It is bad enough to be hit on an empty stomach . . .

Like most managers who know what they are doing, Jim Wicks would leave instructions until last. Pearls of wisdom are intended to stay in a boxer's mind, and the brain is not so receptive when a boxer first returns to his corner. Jim would keep his tactics talking down to a minimum. Two or three salient points or observations - that was all that was necessary.

The third person in the corner, the role that brother George so often filled, is the water carrier and odd-job man. We always used to put household adhesive tape around the outside of the water-bottle to prevent it slipping in anybody's hand, and George would always cover the top of the water-bucket as he carried it to the ringside. There is always the chance that somebody might throw something in it. We haven't a drug problem in British boxing, but nobody takes foolish risks, and the cover stays on the bucket throughout the fight. George always sat with the water-bucket between his knees, and so does any sensible corner man.

The second and corner man do not see a lot of the fight. They are kept too busy between intervals. In my case, while I was trying not to take more punishment, Danny would be replacing his swab sticks, topping up the adrenalin and smearing on more Vaseline. George would be refilling the water-bottle and cleaning the bowl I'd used for gargling.

Boxing people are versatile. Promoters can be matchmakers; managers can become chief advisers at the ringside, where the trainer's role is usually that of chief second. But there are two exceptions. The referee and the timekeeper.

ROUND 8

Referees and Time-Keepers

Boxers often have their heads examined, for the best of reasons. But I don't recall a referee being submitted to the same procedure. I think they should. I might then be able to discover why they do it. It can't be for the money. The cash they get, in Britain, for all that aggravation, is paid in accordance with a scale based on the cost of the promotion. In the days when a typical middle-of-the-road bill could be put together for between £2,500 and £4,000, the Class 'A' man would receive £30 and the Class 'B' man £17.50.

The cash has improved since, with inflation, but so has the cost of living. But donning the white shirt, bow tie and dark trousers is not exactly a short-cut along the road to riches. The time-keeper, the right-hand man of the referee, fares no better. Like a lot of folk in boxing, referees and time-keepers are in the game because they like it. There can't be any other reason. When was the last time a boxing crowd rose to its feet and cheered and clapped the referee? When was the last time they chucked abuse and sometimes more tangible objects at the poor official? The answer to the first question is: Can't remember. And to the second: Last week.

I have never been tempted to become a referee. But I can't deny that it is an ego trip for some old boxers who like the limelight and still want their share. I do not mean that as a slight on their integrity, but as some slight explanation of why some old professionals become Third Men.

It is a contrary life, that of a boxing referee. At the start, it is a lot of fun, going around the various halls and meeting any number of people. But as the referee climbs the ladder, the more aloof he has to become until, at the top, the star men are on nodding terms with no one but themselves. It has to be that way. The blokes who handle the big fights and the championship bouts cannot afford to be too friendly with boxers and their managers. The nudge, nudge, wink, wink brigade would soon make plenty out of that.

How does a man become a boxing referee? He asks for it – in more ways than one. More often than not, if he hasn't fought professionally, he comes from a boxing background or, having done his stuff with an amateur club, he decides to make the change.

Mike Jacobs, who spends his working life in London's West End as the sales director of a firm of insurance brokers, is one of Britain's best-known and most respected officials, always in demand for world title fights that do not involve British boxers. Mike's father promoted in London's East End, he boxed in the boys' clubs and decided, at the ripe old age of twenty-two, to go in for refereeing.

Mike, like any other applicant, met members of the Boxing Board of Control's referees' committee and, after a general discussion about the boxing game to ensure that all of them were not wasting their time, he was invited to take scoring tests. The would-be referee goes to see fights, sits at the ringside and judges, and then his figures are compared with the official referee's scorecard.

If he shows the right sort of potential, this pattern is continued through thirty to forty fights. Then he is invited to meet the referees' committee, which consists of Star class men, the élite of British referees and normally there are no more than about half a dozen elevated to this particular peerage. This inquisition is designed to test the embryo referee's ability to make decisions quickly. Deliberately, the questions come as thick and fast as situations would arise in the ring.

If the green light comes on, he will be given small fights to handle, even though a licence has not yet been granted. He will be given the bottom-of-the-bill at a small-hall show and officiates with power only to stop the fight if it becomes too one-sided. A knock-out relieves him of the responsibility of deciding a verdict, but if a fight goes all the way, a judge, sitting incognito outside the ring, gives the appropriate nod, although the referee inside the ring announces the result.

It was at this period of his career that Mike Jacobs, after a working day, would spend evenings in gymnasiums like the Thomas A'Beckett, offering to referee training bouts. There was a two-fold advantage to be gained from this. Not only did it give Mike experience, it got the two boxers, novices more often than not, accustomed to boxing with a third man in the ring.

That was the time when Jacobs had friends in every boxing camp, but now that he is established he makes it a hard and fast rule not only to be careful in his social conversations with boxers and managers but to strike gaming clubs, betting shops and racecourses, etc., from his visiting list.

It might be argued that the use of novice referees is not fair on the fighters. I don't agree. There is only one place where a referee can gain experience, and that is inside the ring. He must start in there sometime. The judge outside is sufficient protection and, until somebody comes up with a better idea, I'll go along with the system. After all, the boxers are novices, too, hardly fighting for massive purses, and in any case, Control Board records ensure that even the young fighter bumps into the young referee only rarely.

Licences are issued by the area committees of the Boxing Board of Control, and Mike Jacobs received his after two or three shows. He was a Class 'B' referee, licensed for twelve months, and could control fights of up to twenty-four minutes, eight-rounders that is. Jacobs' 'B' licence was confirmed after a year, and he was on his way. But promotion can never be quick. In addition to the few Star class referees, there are normally between ten and fifteen Class 'A' officials and some thirty in the 'B' grade. Class 'B' referees can apply for re-grading after three years, but of course their licences can be withdrawn if their standard falls. Jacobs took eleven years to reach 'A' grading and only two more to reach Star status. Class 'A' referees can take all fights except eliminators for national titles and the championship bouts themselves, for national and world titles. The Star man can take any bout.

Once a referee is confirmed as Class 'B', he hasn't much else to learn, technically. All he wants now is experience and nimble footwork with which to dodge the missiles! But, seriously, there are two ways in which the inexperienced referee can make an impression. His first duty is always to the welfare of the boxers in the ring with him. Secondly, he can make such a difference to them if he officiates with a smile on his face. The fighters are tense enough. Understandably. But, if the referee allows tension to show in his face, it will not be long before the boxers lose confidence in him.

My views on the subject of judges are well-known. I am against them. But at least some progress was made in the summer of 1981 when both world bodies in the United States, the World Boxing Association and the World Boxing Council, decided on two scoring judges outside the ring and the referee also scoring. Previously, the WBC operated with a non-scoring referee inside the ring merely controlling the contest, and three scoring judges on the other side of the ropes.

A good referee can help to make a nice fight. He must be unobtrusive, and completely in charge. Jacobs and the rest of our Star men are adept at giving the boxers confidence, and the words of wisdom before the first bell can make all the difference. Contrary to what might be expected, the referee does not go to the dressing-rooms before the fight, unless it is an international contest, when an interpreter helps to ensure that both boxers are fully conversant with what they can and cannot do.

Mind you, the words don't always sink in, especially when our British boys are involved on the Continent. Most of my mementoes have gone now, nearly all of them donated to charitable causes, but I keep one as a reminder of a huge Italian named Piero Tomasoni who was known in his own locality as the Axeman of Manerbio. The souvenir is a boxer's foul cup, made of aluminium and foam padding, which is supposed to stop you getting hurt if an illegal blow should make contact with the lower part of the body.

Piero heard the rules being intoned, but didn't get the message. I put him down for a count of eight in the first round, then he went berserk and we had a bit of a brawl. Piero tossed science out of the window and threw his punches anywhere. The middle of the foul cup is something like seven inches below my navel. It is convex, the same shape as the lower part of the stomach. When I took it off, it had three dents right in the centre, and was concave. I'd had it thirteen years, too.

I can't imagine the Mike Jacobs class of referee allowing that sort of thing to happen, but no official is without his blind side, no matter if he does develop a touch of the Fred Astaires. Boxers have ways and means of roughing each other up – it isn't a game for angels – and the good referee will clamp down on them, *if* he spots the offences. It is not always easy.

One of the favourite tricks, usually brought to Britain by visiting Americans, is the thumb in the eye. It smarts, it waters, and you don't see the next punch coming. Then there is the inside of the glove, which becomes surprisingly rough when it is rubbed down the front of your face.

A recent innovation, legalised by the New York State Athletic Commission in 1981, is the glove without a thumb. This is an idea that has been touted around for a fair while, and I saw a couple of early examples. I wasn't impressed by them, but this latest glove is different. With my track record, I have to be in favour of a glove that reduces cuts around the eyes, and not even the sharpest operator can gouge without a thumb. They use the new gloves in all bouts in New York State, except those in which a title is at stake.

A hand round the back of an opponent's neck is quite useful for pulling him on to a Sunday punch. So is a foot on an opponent's instep when he is trying to back off.

The pre-fight lecture over - and often it is not much more than a reminder about going to a neutral corner at knock-downs ... clean break at the clinches, and so on - the referee glances at the time-keeper and indicates that he is ready to start. Comes the call of 'Seconds Out', and the fight is on.

Which brings me to one of boxing's anomalies. Once the fight has started, there is not supposed to be even a cough from the corners. If there is any signalling or shouting, the rules of boxing are being broken and the referee has the power, after a warning, to order the offender from the corner for the rest of the fight.

Anybody who hasn't broken this rule hasn't been in boxing longer than one fight. Human nature being what it is, it is impossible for someone in a boxer's corner to watch his man belting or being belted without reacting. The fans are not exactly models of decorum either. I don't see that the rule serves any purpose, and I reckon that if a boxer can take notice of what is going on in his corner, he isn't concentrating on the fight as much as he should be. The only exceptional circumstance is when the boxer is in trouble. I reckon that is one time when he can be forgiven for not concentrating.

Perhaps the referees have most of the fun in boxing. Mike Jacobs, who officiates in a distinctive velvet jacket, has had the ring lights go out on him and the ring collapse underneath him, but his favourite story is of the night he nearly knocked out a fighter.

The venue was the Colston Hall, Bristol, where the ring usually has to be erected over auditorium steps. There is no difficulty. It means that there is a short drop one side and a hell of a deep one on the other side.

It was back in Mike's days as a Class 'B' referee, and he

had spent far too long on a heavyweight novices fight which had gone the distance. Most of the time, Mike had been pushing and heaving, trying to unclinch around thirty stone of man and muscle. Next on were a couple of flyweights. They, too, were tangled in a clinch, so Mike went in to prise them apart. Unfortunately, his heels and instep caught, and in any case he hadn't adjusted from mauling the heavies about. An almighty shove pitched one of the flyweights half-way through the ropes on the long drop side. Fortunately, Mike managed to retain a hold and dragged him back into the ring.

By the way, if you imagine you see Mike Jacobs working in boxing boots instead of the usual pumps or light shoes, don't be surprised. Resin, which they used to spread over the floor to help a boxer's grip, is on the way out. Boxing boots with pimpled soles, similar to golf shoes with their adhesive qualities, are on the way in. Normal leather soles get too shiny, hence Jacobs' decision, as he can't beat them, to join them.

Once the bout has started, the time-keeper comes into his own. One of the best-known is dear old Tom Powell, a florist from Croydon, Surrey. He started back in 1948, and was at the ringside when I fought Muhammad Ali for the world title. Back in the thirties welterweight Tom had thirty-six professional fights with what he calls mixed results. He was paid ten shillings (fifty pence) for the first and £7.50 for the last. He got into boxing by accident. He thought he was attending a physical fitness clinic. They told him to put on a pair of gloves and two seconds later he was picking himself off the floor. He has been in the game ever since.

Like everybody else in boxing, time-keepers are licensed, and most of them are veterans like Tom, who won the British Empire Medal while serving as a Royal Air Force physical training instructor during the war.

Time-keepers are required to work with two watches, which they buy themselves. Perfectionist Tom uses three – one that runs for four minutes, and two that time the split-seconds. The time-keeper clocks the rounds and the intervals, and comes into his own when there is a knock-down. He starts to count as soon as the boxer hits the canvas, and the referee picks up the count from the time-keeper, for the benefit of the stricken boxer. They call in unison until they reach ten. The time-keeper calls 'Ten', and the referee uses the word 'Out'.

If they fail to get it right, there is chaos of the Fred Karno kind which made a farce of the return fight between Sonny Liston and Muhammad Ali for the world heavyweight title fight in 1965, though nobody thought it funny at the time.

The referee was former world heavyweight champion Jersey Joe Walcott, a particular favourite of mine. But although Jersey Joe was the people's choice, he wasn't a vastly experienced referee. As we know, Liston was a bit slow out of his corner and Ali whacked him. Instead of going to a neutral corner, Ali stood over Sonny. Walcott tried to move him by force and then remembered the count. The time-keeper then informed Walcott that as the count had started when Liston dropped to the canvas and had now reached twenty-two, Sonny could be considered k.o.'d - twice over. But when Walcott turned round to proclaim Ali the winner, Liston was on his feet, and heading for his opponent. A couple of perfunctory punches were exchanged before Liston accepted the inevitable.

It is vital that there are no misunderstandings between referee and time-keeper at the end of rounds. If the time-keeper signals the end of the round when the count is on, the bout is over if the stricken boxer fails to rise before 'ten' is reached. If he manages to get up and beat the count, his corner have the rest of the interval in which to attempt to revive him. This does not apply at the end of the last round. Then, the count ceases at the final bell, when it is possible that the boxer on the canvas can be the winner on points. After all, he hasn't been knocked out during the duration of the fight.

Ali should have heeded the lesson of Jack Dempsey, who failed to regain his world heavyweight title from Gene Tunney in what boxing historians now call the Battle of the Long Count. On this occasion, the confusion was not the fault of the time-keeper. The great Dempsey was his own worst enemy.

Tunney had taken Dempsey's title from him in September 1926, on a points decision. Exactly a year later, they faced each other again, and both boxers had agreed that, in the event of a knock-down, the other would retire to the farthest corner. Dempsey put Tunney on the floor in the seventh round but delayed going to the corner. So the referee, Dave Barry, refused to start the count until he did. Tunney climbed to his feet fourteen seconds after being put down and went on to gain another points decision. The curious feature of both Dempsey–Tunney scraps was that they were made over ten rounds instead of the then customary, and now statutory, fifteen rounds.

Time-keeper Tom Powell's favourite yarn climaxes with his telling HRH the Duke of Edinburgh to keep quiet. The Duke was talking to Sir Charles Forte at the National Sporting Club, where the rule calls for silence while the boxers are in action.

My favourite is of Tom arriving at a tournament venue before the official inspector from the Boxing Board of Control and finding an assured young lady in the dressing-room. It was before the Control Board took over the responsibility for all medical appointments at tournaments. The local hospital had been requested to supply an off-duty doctor, and they had. Neither posterity nor Tom's records, reveal the number of knock-outs that night.

I suppose we have progressed since the early twenties, when a number of American big-name boxers took their own referee around with them. Jack Dempsey was one of them, but when you think about it, who would argue with the Manassa Mauler in his prime?

Dempsey also did well out of refereeing. He ran the world middleweight title fight between Ceferino Garcia and Glen Lee in Manila, and then did a non-title bout between Sixto Escobar, the Puerto Rican who was world bantamweight champion, and Simon Chevez. Jack picked up more than $10,000 for each of them, and that was in the late thirties. Joe Louis picked up a similar sized jackpot when he needed it, by refereeing the Joe Frazier–Jerry Quarry fight in 1974 – which, if nothing else, underlines the size of Dempsey's fees.

Meanwhile, our British referees will carry on earning more modest purses and retiring, according to rule, when they are sixty-five years of age. Between times they will report the disqualification of any boxer to the promoter immediately and to the Board of Control within twenty-four hours.

They signify the winner of a fight by walking across to the boxer and raising his hand. In the event of a draw the hands of both boxers are raised. They decide whether or not a blow is a foul on their own experience, without consulting medical opinion.

If the time-keeper is taken ill, they stop the contest until another official has been appointed and use their own discretion in deciding whether to restart or declare the partly-contested round complete. They will, if they injure themselves or are taken ill, allow the time-keeper to stop the contest and retire in favour of another official who will use both cards, the uncompleted round having been restarted, with which to judge the contest.

They are duty bound not to canvass any person to obtain employment in boxing, either verbally or by correspondence. Finally, they learn to cope with all those other people who never see a bout the same way as the man in charge.

For their benefit, I mark a card. Points are awarded for clean punches with the knuckle part of the glove. So, obviously, the boxer who delivers most of these has to be the winner.

In each round, a boxer is awarded a maximum of ten points

– it used to be five. If both men score well, the round could be marked 10–10. More usually, it is 10–9 or 10–8, and rarely wider than 10–7. Marks can be earned for good defence, including slipping and ducking, but the boxer who is continuously going forward must have his initiative rewarded.

I must warn fans that excitement can blind them. A lad can look in excellent nick when he is throwing punches from all over the place. But what I, and the referee, always look for is how many are landing on the head and body and therefore scoring, and how many are being taken on the arms or by the gloves.

If anybody is wondering why some of the older boxers appear to be advantageously treated, it is probably because their powers of recovery are known, and those of a youngster are not.

Referees and time-keepers are the taken-for-granted men of boxing who do not have a lot going for them. But there is one sweetener I haven't mentioned, and it is appreciated. Wherever they go in the world, the counts are always in English. 'Seven ... eight ... nine ... Out' is a universal language.

ROUND 9

Equipment

I love looking at old boxing paintings and pictures. I have a selection on the wall at home, and they serve as a constant reminder that a sport which can, at times, be so brutal, also has a nobility that makes it unique.

One of my favourites is a tint depicting Jack Broughton, the father of British boxing, squaring up to a cold-eyed character named George Stevenson. They met in 1741, and the scene portrays boxing at its most basic. Two men, each committed to being a winner. Each knows that one of them has to be beaten, but each is certain that *he* isn't destined to be the loser.

There is a grandeur about them and, but for an ominous sense of foreboding, they could be knights without the shining armour.

Nothing much has changed in the intervening two hundred years or so. They are wearing buckled shoes instead of boots. Long stockings are pulled up over trousers to just below the knee. A sash around the waist is not a suggestion of cavalier tendencies. It would mop up the sweat, just as the modern waistband does. Boxing gear has not undergone a transformation. It has merely evolved.

That confrontation between Broughton and Yorkshireman Stevenson changed the course of boxing history. It lasted thirty-five minutes before Stevenson was knocked out by a blow near the heart. He died a few days later, and soon afterwards Broughton introduced his Rules for the Prize Ring.

Broughton must have been brighter than the average pugilist of his time. He opened Broughton's Academy, and taught the gentry and their sons the art of self-defence. But the young bloods didn't take kindly to having their features re-arranged by sets of hefty knuckles. After indulging in the masculinity of Broughton's establishment, they were none too happy at looking below their best when confronting their ladies later in the day. Young bloods haven't changed!

So Broughton invented 'mufflers', which protected the fists and, more importantly, the face. I know whom to thank for the good looks I have today. However, Broughton's gloves were used only for sparring in the Academy. When the chips were down, it was back to bare knuckles. No way was a fighter of those days going to risk having the Michael extracted by charges of being effeminate. It was, and still is, a man's game.

No reference to gloves found its way into official documents until the Marquess of Queensberry drew up his guidelines in the 1860s. Even then they were banned for championship bouts. When they were worn, gloves weighed only five ounces, and were not as popular as 'kid gloves', which could be skin-tight and weighed only two ounces. Kid gloves must have been better than nothing, though if boxers had been wearing them in my day, I would rather have been on the giving than the receiving end. I reckon I could spread somebody's nose just as far with kid gloves as bare fists, but I would be surprised if I damaged my knuckles quite as much.

However, civilisation overtakes us all, including boxing. John L. Sullivan, an Irish-American who was born in Boston, reigned as the last world heavyweight champion of the prize-fighting era, roistering his whisky-consuming way from 1882, when he knocked out Paddy Ryan in nine rounds, until 1892, when Gentleman Jim Corbett, from San Francisco, knocked out Sullivan in the twenty-first round of the first world heavyweight championship bout fought in gloves.

Anybody who thinks that tough by modern standards should be pointed in the direction of John L.'s previous defence three years earlier, the last of the bare-knuckle title punch-ups. Sullivan was then coming up to thirty-one years of age but, having purged his system of whisky, he fought Jake Kilrain. It lasted two hours, sixteen minutes and twenty-three seconds before Kilrain was counted out – in round seventy-five. Gloves could hardly come soon enough, even if they were mostly of the five-ounce variety. Today, professional boxers in Britain use either six- or eight-ounce gloves according to their weight, and ten-ounce gloves in training to avoid doing too much damage to each other. Amateur boxers, except in junior contests, wear eight-ounce gloves, the same weight as in most of America – apart from the heavyweight division in which they all wear ten-ounce gloves.

Around the turn of the century, when more and more fighters scorned bare knuckles, gloves were made of horse hair. Now, it is a mixture of synthetic rubber and horse hair. Most of the glove is rubber-packed, but we haven't yet found anything better than horse hair to do the shaping.

Gloves can burst under pressure. It happened, readers might recall, to an opponent of mine named Cassius Clay.

I've seen the film of the fight often enough. But nothing changes my conviction that I would have had every chance of winning that fight had the interval between the fourth and fifth rounds not been extended while they tried to rectify the damage to Clay's glove. How it was damaged is a different tale, depending on from which side of the fence it is told.

The year was 1963 – the venue Wembley Stadium. Clay (the Muhammad Ali was not to come until 1964) was heading up the world rankings, fairly obviously destined for the top, though I wouldn't have said that before we fought. He had never been put on the canvas and, despite his pre-match boasts, for publicity purposes, that he was going to finish me in five, I was able to dig the left hook into him near the end of the fourth round to drop him on the deck. He had slit my left eyebrow in the third; I was donating blood to half of the ringside; and if I was going to win, I had to do it quickly.

I thumped him about five seconds before the end of the round. Luckily for Clay, he was on the ropes, and he slid off them to the floor. Had he been in the middle of the ring when I nailed him, he would have gone like a sack of potatoes and have hurt himself more than he did. But he was starting to get to his feet when the bell went to indicate the end of the round. So I was unlucky on two counts. It was a pity I didn't get 'Enery's 'Ammer in a few seconds earlier, and it was a pity that when I did Clay had the ropes to help him.

I don't know how badly Clay was hurt. To be quite honest, I was having troubles of my own. Niagara had turned red. But Angelo Dundee, the genius who guided Clay, had his own ideas. I'm told Angelo broke a sprint record getting across to Clay, and from my corner, when Danny Holland had staunched the flow of blood, I could see that Clay wasn't enjoying life.

Suddenly, there was all hell let loose in Clay's corner. Stewards were called, referee Tommy Smith was walking over, and they were all inspecting a split in Clay's right glove. How it got there was one of life's little mysteries, but there was a huge lump of stuffing gone, too. By the time they had tried, unsuccessfully, to find the spare pair of gloves that should have been available, and returned to the ringside, a hell of a lot of time had gone by, and the fight had to be restarted with Clay having had about a minute and three-quarters to recover from the knock-down.

That glove was so bad it could have scoured clean a burnt saucepan. After two or three punches of the fifth round, Clay had found the target, the waterfall of blood was back, and I was gone – in no state to continue. I was literally blinded by my own blood. I couldn't see. I often wonder what became of that glove. I must ask Angelo some time.

The surface of the modern boxing glove is leather. The laces are always tied and knotted on the back of the hand, and then covered by an elastic sleeve. Gloves haven't any special lasting qualities. It depends how much they are used. Clay seemed to get through them quicker than most.

Underneath the gloves are the bandages and tape. Boxers are allowed only so much of each, as laid down in the Rules of Boxing at the end of this book. The bandage goes round the back of the hand, the palm and the wrist, and not between the fingers or the thumb. Tape goes on top of the bandage and between the fingers.

It is not the fingers which take the strain. The back of the hand does, because correct punches are delivered with the knuckle, and if the hands and wrists were not bandaged, each impact would spread the flesh. At the end of a fight the hands would be a mass of bruises.

Boxers have a thing about bandaging. Most of them do it themselves. Jim Wicks used to say that bandaging was like buying a pair of shoes. Nobody can do it for you. Once, in my novice days, Danny Holland had showed me the best way to do the job – it was mine and nobody else's, even for training. Yes, a boxer does bandage even for sparring and punch-bag work. After all, he is trying to simulate actual fight conditions, and fighting is all about delivering a punch as hard as you can. I had sparring partners, some of them well-paid, who quit. I don't suppose there is a successful boxer who hasn't had the same experience.

It would take me about twenty minutes to bandage. That was about par for the course, but some fighters are incredibly meticulous. Paul Pender, the American who lost his world middleweight crown to Terry Downes, Britain's favourite boxing character of his day, at Wembley in 1961, was one of the worst. That was a bout that very nearly didn't come off. With less than an hour to go to the bell, there was an almighty wrangle in Pender's dressing-room, the contentious issue being the amount of tape and bandage Pender wanted to use.

Pender had brittle hands, so it doesn't take a clairvoyant to discover what it was all about. Boxers, managers, trainers, Control Board officials and even Pender's lawyer hammered away at each other for about thirty-five minutes before a formula was agreed upon, and I believe that at one stage Pender threatened to call off the fight. In the event, the American retired after the ninth round, pleading a combination of stomach trouble and a couple of nicks under the eyes. But Pender is among those who would never under-estimate the importance of bandaging.

Neither would some of the old-time fighters. A favourite gag, after the hands had been covered, was to dip them in plaster of paris powder before putting on the gloves. Between rounds the second would make sure that plenty of water was sponged down his boxer's arms to trickle into the glove and mix with the powder. That is why, in these more enlightened days, bandages have to be stamped in the dressing-room by an official before the gloves can be put on. At title fights, the gloves are put on in the ring so that everybody can see what is going on. It is a long while since a horseshoe found its way into a glove!

Beneath the shorts, a boxer wears a jock-strap and a protector. The reasons for both are obvious, and I have already told the tale of Tomasoni and the protector. That has its funny side, but the protector is a very serious piece of equipment. Nor is it a modern innovation. Jack Johnson, the first negro to win the world heavyweight championship – he was Number 1 between 1908 and 1915 – wore one, though I doubt whether his was made of aluminium, as they are today. Aluminium is light, but though a dent can be pressed by a single finger, it will take the normal punch without bending.

Shorts and socks are a matter of personal choice. Comfort is the main requirement. As we went into the eighties, long shorts became the fashion. I think they came back with the advent of Joe Frazier, who succeeded Ali as world champion until George Foreman had him down six times in two rounds in 1973. I suppose Smokin' Joe would be the first to admit that it doesn't really matter what length your shorts are if you

At a tribute to the late Jack Solomons in 1980 with, from left to right, Dave Charnley, Jack Petersen, Charlie Nash and Howard Winstone.

Six British champions who all held European titles at the same time, in 1974. From left to right: Ken Buchanan (lightweight), Kevin Finnegan (middleweight), Joe Bugner (heavyweight), John H. Stracey (welterweight), Johnny Clark (bantamweight) and John Conteh (light-heavyweight).

I was honoured to be asked to present the BBC's 1971 Sports Personality of the Year trophy to Her Royal Highness Princess Anne, an expert horsewoman.

Banging a mean drum is former world middleweight champion Alan Minter. The group were named Jigsaw and they were recording a disc called 'Prize Fighter' for a film about the life of Minter. Now that never happened to me. . . .

At a television quiz show, in the exalted company of former England footballers Bobby Charlton, Gordon Banks and Keith Newton, and (*centre*) the BBC's Stuart Hall.

The author with film star Robert Stack at a pro-celebrity golf tournament.

Terry Downes, the former world middleweight champion from Paddington, turned actor when his fighting days were over. Who better to play the tough sergeant in Sean O'Casey's *The Shadow of a Gunman*?

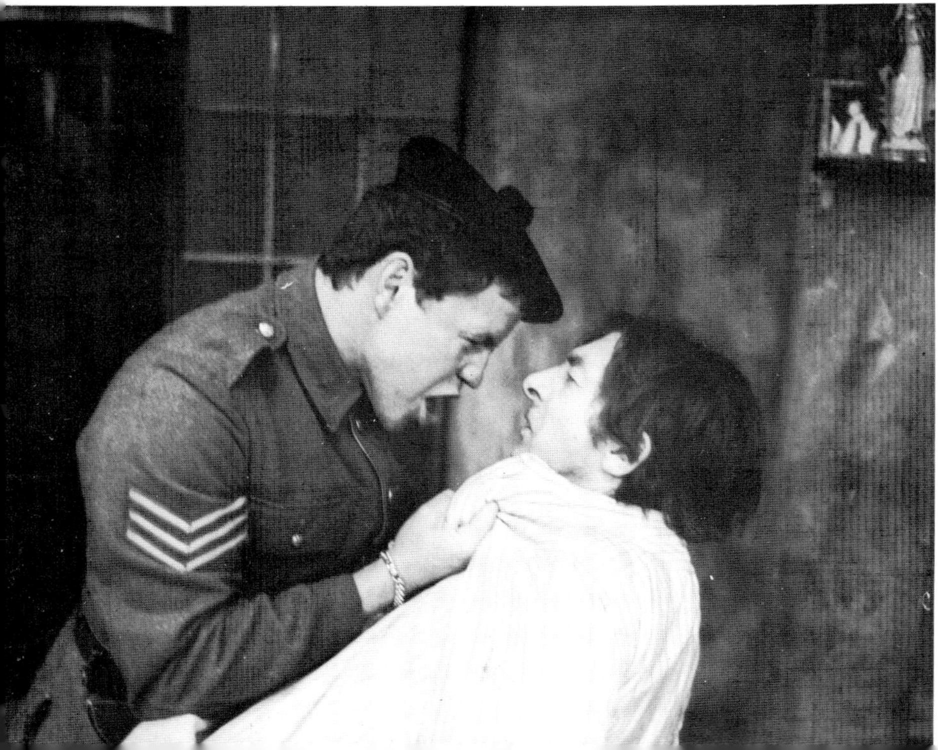

Swingin'. Jersey Joe Walcott, the former world heavyweight champion, who has devoted so much of his time to children.

Like many a fighter before him, former world champion Joe Frazier went into show business when he hung up his gloves. Not surprisingly, the entertainment, which toured Europe as well as the United States, was called the Joe Frazier Show.

Another side of the talented Jim Watt. Normally the Scotsman plays a guitar, but here he shows enough skill on the piano to impress bandleader James Last.

Pop singer Billy Joel, who was a formidable welterweight before quitting the boxing game for show business. He won 20 out of 22 professional fights. Doing the honours are Colin Power (*left*), former commonwealth champion, and three of Britain's former world champions, Alan Minter, John H. Stracey and Terry Downes.

Terry Lawless, who took John H. Stracey, Maurice Hope and Jim Watt to world titles, a feat unsurpassed by any other British boxing manager. Watt is on the far left and Hope on the far right.

When Sugar Ray Robinson finished fighting, he took to the stage. A demonstration of footwork among London's daffodils.

are going to spend most of your time in them sprawling on the canvas.

I liked them about three inches above the knee, and my old friend Bernard Hart from Lonsdale Sports, the London boxing equipment specialists, used to have them made specially for me. That is not as egotistical as the layman might think. Anybody who has tried to put on a pair of normal physical training shorts over a boxing protector discovers that he has forgotten something. Boxing shorts have to be shaped.

If socks have sufficient length to get a decent turn-down over the top of boxing boots, that is good enough. I wore football socks more often than not. A thick wool gives a boxer all he needs underfoot. Later, those American tube socks, which just stretch over any size of foot, became the rage, but it might have been no more than a passing fancy.

Boots I had a fad about. I liked to keep the same pair for fighting in. Appearances have to be maintained after all. Once they were broken in, the Number 1 pair were for ring use only. I trained in a different pair. Again, fashion is dictating the length of boot. They are gradually reaching higher up the calf.

As recently as the early seventies, boots were barely covering the shin. In the late thirties they were down where they always had been, barely above the ankle. That was probably a mistake. In more enlightened days we realised that the more support the ankles had, the better.

Most boots are made of chrome-leather and pigskin. But, again, the late seventies and early eighties saw a change. Traditionally, we fought in leather-soled footwear. The leather was roughed up before usage and I maintain we got a perfect grip on resin-sprinkled canvas. The combination of resin, canvas and leather gave me all the adhesion I wanted. Then came the introduction of the ribbed or pimple-soled rubber boots. To me, they don't seem to offer the same strength of grip, but most of the younger boxers are going for them.

As resin gradually fills the gaps between the pimples, the modern boots lose their effectiveness. How long, I wonder, before we have to make the big decision – pimples or resin? I don't think boxing can have both. The pimple-soled boots will become cheaper – an important point with the amateur boxers. As there will be no necessity for resin, I suppose pimples will win in the long term.

But no matter which combination of boots and socks I wore, there was always one consistent sequel. After every fight I would have a blood blister under the big toe of my right foot. That was where I got all my leverage. So the moral is that any boxer who wants to know whether he is punching properly has only to look under his big toe.

One more item, and the boxer is ready to go into the ring. He requires a gum-shield, without which his top and bottom teeth are likely to do a mischief to his tongue. By common consent, Ted 'Kid' Lewis, who was born Solomon Mendeloff in London's East End and disputed the world welterweight championship with Irish-American Jack Britton between 1915 and 1921, was the first man to wear them. And I used to get mine from the same fellow, Jack Marks, a dentist in London's Notting Hill.

They are made from natural latex or vulcanised rubber, and they should be made individually. I would pop down to Jack Marks; he'd take an impression, and inside about a fortnight I would have a new gum-shield. They last about a year, because the sensible boxer also uses them in training. In fact, a common sight in most gyms is a row of jars with what seems to be a chorus line of teeth grinning in the sunlight. They are the gum-shields, labelled and soaking in antiseptic, awaiting their owners' arrival.

Any boxer doubting the wisdom of wearing gum-shields should ponder the fate of Stanley Ketchel, who was knocked out by Jack Johnson in the twelfth round of a world heavyweight title fight in 1909. Ketchel finished the pounding with two teeth fewer than he had when he went into the ring. How are we so sure? Because they were found embedded in one of Johnson's gloves.

Boxers need somewhere to fight, and that is why we have this square we call a ring. I have heard various explanations for this, but the theory most widely accepted goes, predictably, back to the days of bare-knuckle prize-fighting.

The boxers worked in pairs, travelling up and down the country visiting the fairgrounds and village greens. There they would gather onlookers round them in a circle. Having previously prepared a loop of rope, members of the circle would then hold it taut, and so the ring was formed. Eventually, the crowds were too big for a circle, and, in any case, the excitement of what they were watching frequently made spectators forget to hang on to the rope.

So the rope became a square with stakes at the corners and, in good time, there appeared three horizontal ropes at each side, just as we have them today. In the summer of 1981, the World Boxing Council, which governs the sport in certain areas of the United States, decided to opt for a four-roped square, but I don't think the rest of the world is all that keen to follow suit. WBC say there is less likelihood of a man falling out of a four-roped arena, but how often do boxers hurtle through the ropes anyway? There might be less resilience with a four-roped ring, which would make it harder for a boxer under pressure to use the ropes as he can now. But that is all part of boxing, and I would hate to see it go.

I only remember putting one guy through the ropes, and it would have to be my great pal Joe Erskine. We had met four times as amateurs, and he had stuffed me twice as a professional. At Earl's Court, London, in May 1959, former champion Joe challenged for his old British and Empire titles which I'd nicked from Brian London.

I went after him in the opening round, and kept the pressure up right through the fight. Eventually, I caught him with a series of punches including the left hook when he was going down. Poor Joe pitched through the middle and bottom ropes and sprawled with his back arched. I really thought he had broken his back. Fortunately for all of us, there was room for Joe's body to go through the ropes. Had there been four ropes, I wonder whether his neck and shoulders might not have been twisted up among what would have to be the bottom two ropes.

The floor of the ring must be of canvas, with a safety mat beneath it, and the promoter needs to satisfy the Boxing Board of Control on this safety factor. The corner posts must be padded and the ropes bandaged, to prevent a boxer being burned across the back. The ropes must be taut, and I always used to try and make a point of leaning against them before the bout began, just to see how much 'give' there was in them.

The most important feature of any ring is its size. The minimum is fourteen feet square, and the maximum is twenty feet, and anybody who thinks it is all as simple as that is deluding himself.

For a start, take the dinner show tournament. Any self-respecting promoter will want the ring as small as possible. Nothing to do with the fighters. He wants more tables, meaning more diners to buy his food and his wine. The boxers don't even make first base on the priorities list.

But there are times when boxers get their priorities right, and that is when they are world champions. The champ calls the shots. What he says goes, and the promoter plays ball. That's business, the boxing business.

Two of the greatest champions, Rocky Marciano and Muhammad Ali, demanded, and got, rings of extreme sizes. Rocky had only one style of fighting, and that was to keep on windmilling punches until the other fellow dropped with exhaustion. Rocky, who was killed when his aircraft crashed on the eve of his forty-sixth birthday, wasn't called the Brockton Blockbuster for nothing. Science and Rocky weren't even on nodding terms. Naturally, Rocky wanted the ring as small as possible. He didn't want to spend time chasing opponents.

Ali – 'dance like a butterfly, sting like a bee', he used to say – liked all the space he could find. He wanted the wide open spaces, and was a hell of an opponent to catch up with.

All world title fights now have to be in an eighteen-foot minimum ring, which wouldn't have suited Rocky at all. Nor was promoter Harry Levene too pleased to discover that the Wembley ring, when he hosted the 1981 world lightweight championship match between Jim Watt and Alexis Arguello, was smaller than regulations. It was a last-minute discovery, too, and there was a rush of carpentry activity carried out at a furious pace.

When I fought Ali for the world title at Arsenal's football ground, we tried to have the ring as small as we could. After all, it was going to have to be built on site, and a small ring was my best chance of catching up with him. Was he having any? Not likely. The ultimatum was loud and positive. Roughly translated, it became: 'Twenty feet or no fight.'

In the bare-knuckle days, rings were between twenty and twenty-four feet square. In amateur boxing, they can be between twelve and twenty feet, a range which has to include juniors as well as seniors.

For training use, a boxer will want track-suits, sweat-shirts etc. for gym activities, and a head-guard. I know boxers who won't wear a head-guard when training or sparring. They argue that it gives them so much protection that it makes them careless. Well, good luck to them, but I would never agree. A fight postponed because of a training incident spells nothing but aggravation to everybody – even the caterers and the local bus company.

But I would never go along with those do-gooders who suggest that boxers should be made to wear head-guards at the fight itself. It is a man's game, is boxing, and I'd rather see the cotton-wool left in the dressing-room. Apart from that factor, there is slight danger from the fact that head-guards are not made to measure. They can't be. We all have heads of a different size. It is the strap that adjusts the head-guard, not the head-guard that fits. If the strap slips, they are immediately ill-fitting, and it is not unknown for an ear to be cut in the gym. That is not so serious, because the action can be stopped.

Jack Dempsey, in the twenties, was one of the first to use a head-guard in the gym. And that's where they ought to stay. Amateurs in the United States Services, and amateurs in Canada and Sweden box in head-guards. I don't quarrel with that. Punch for fun is the name of their pleasure. Professional boxing, as I've said before, is a business.

ROUND 10

The Weight Divisions

When weight limits were first introduced, there were just three divisions. Boxers were either heavyweight, middleweight or lightweight. Now there are ten standard weights in the British Boxing Board of Control's book of regulations, and eleven in the scale recognised by the European Boxing Union and the World Boxing Association. Before we go any farther, this is how the British authority's scale is laid down:

Heavyweight	Any weight
Light-heavyweight	12 st 7 lbs and under
Middleweight	11 st 6 lbs and under
Light-middleweight	11 st and under
Welterweight	10 st 7 lbs and under
Light-welterweight	10 st and under
Lightweight	9 st 9 lbs and under
Featherweight	9 st and under
Bantamweight	8 st 6 lbs and under
Flyweight	8 st and under

The EBU and WBA inserted a junior-lightweight division at 9 st 4 lbs, and there has since emerged the light-feather or super-bantamweight at up to 8 st 10 lbs and light-flyweight at up to 7 st 10 lbs. There are a lot of little blokes in the Far East and Pacific islands, and it is only a matter of time before those weights are on the statute books.

Most senior amateur weights are a pound or two higher, more in the light-heavy and heavy grades, because amateurs are not encouraged to fight at anything other than their natural weight. Wasting to make weight and punching for fun do not go together. But what wheeling and dealing the professionals have done on the way to stabilising the present accepted code. Back to the beginning. . . .

The bare-knuckle boys gave nothing away, unless it was a hefty smack in the chops, so many poor characters back in the old bruising days had no chance of winning. With only the heavy, middle and light divisions, the range between the tops and bottoms of each was too great. Imagine, say, Alan Minter, the former world middleweight champion, scaling a few pounds over the 11 st 6 lbs mark and tangling with a 16 st Muhammad Ali. The only thing to bet on would be the round in which Minter would take the count.

Fortunately for the future of boxing, the shrewdies who count the cash put on their thinking caps. With only three weights there were only three titles. Nothing sells fight seats better than title fights, so the next move was blindingly predictable. The bantam, feather and welterweight grades were slotted in first, to be followed by the light-heavy and fly.

Yet it wasn't until 1909 that the weights were standardised. They varied all over the world until the National Sporting Club, in London's Covent Garden, fixed the poundages. The basic eight weights were further sub-divided when it was discovered that, with gaps of around half a stone between the weights, some fighters were taking off too much to box successfully at the lower end or giving away too many pounds to opponents in the higher division.

One of the first to benefit from the introduction of the light-heavyweight class was Bob Fitzsimmons, the only English-born fighter to become world heavyweight champion, and the first man to be world title-holder at three weights – in his case middle, light-heavy and heavy. The middle came first, in 1891, when Fitzsimmons knocked out the original Jack Dempsey in the thirteenth round. In 1897, he knocked out James J. Corbett in the fourteenth to be hailed the heavyweight king. Then in 1903, he took the cruiserweight crown from George Gardner by outpointing him over twenty rounds. And thereby hangs the tale.

The campaign to launch the light-heavyweight division was begun by an American boxing promoter and manager named Lou Houseman. He had a good fighter called Jack Root, but the trouble with Root was his weight – only a few pounds more than the middleweight limit. There was another problem in those turn-of-the-century times – the heavyweight champion was the fearsome James J. Jeffries, who was 6 ft $2\frac{1}{2}$ ins tall and usually weighed in at about 15 st 10 lbs.

Houseman got to work. As well as being a promoter and manager, he was a reporter on a Chicago newspaper. His suggestion didn't lack for publicity, and the new division was established at twelve and a half stone. Kid McCoy and Jack Root met at Detroit in 1903, and Root triumphed on points. After only a few months, Root was knocked out by George Gardner, who then made the mistake of going in with Fitzsimmons. Perhaps Gardner was lulled into a false sense of security by Fitzsimmons' age. He was forty-three. But after years of conceding weight in lumps, Bob took Gardner to the cleaners. He was too brainy by far.

Fitzsimmons was the lightest boxer ever to win the heavyweight championship of the world. When he beat Corbett, he weighed only 12 st 4 lbs.

But even after the National Sporting Club's declaration, all was not peace. Boxers themselves used to manipulate the weights. To emphasise the point that the champ is always in the driving seat, Bob Fitzsimmons, back in 1894, had trouble in making the middleweight limit. So he set it a couple of pounds higher. But in 1912, three years after the National Sporting Club and most of the people running boxing thought they had stopped the chicanery, Willie Ritchie, the lightweight title-holder, was also lifting the limit by two pounds.

For some reason, Britain waited ten years before recognising the light-heavyweight division, and the middle didn't reach its present 11 st 6 lbs until 1915. Fitzsimmons had raised it to 11 st 4 lbs, and there it remained. The World

Boxing Association introduced the junior-middleweight grade in 1962. Britain followed suit, calling it light-middle, in 1973. Welters were around in the 1880s, with the current 10 st 7 lbs being settled on in 1909. The light-welter came to Britain in 1973.

Lightweights abounded at 9 st 7 lbs in the 1860s, but since 1912 it has stayed at Ritchie's 9 st 9 lbs. Featherweights became 9 st in 1901, and bantams 8 st 6 lbs in 1920. Britain created the flyweights, at 8 st, in 1909.

Recently we've had the super-bantam in 1976 and the light-fly for the midgets. There was even an attempt to create a paper-weight division at 6 st 11 lbs and upwards, but I reckoned that one got clobbered when they realised they would have to issue all the spectators with binoculars.

What happens at the weigh-in when a boxer is overweight? He has an hour to beat the scales. If he loses the battle, the fight can go on at catch-weights, but the offender will be disciplined. If it is a title fight, then it ceases to be for a championship. In fact, if the offender is the champion, then he automatically forfeits his title.

Benny Lynch, the fiery Glasgow flyweight, lost his world crown that way. He won it in September 1935 by knocking out Jackie Brown of Manchester in two rounds. Total recognition came his way eighteen months later when he outpointed the Philipino, Small Montana. Benny was feted in Glasgow. There wasn't a door his face wouldn't open. Benny liked the good life, and enjoyed it to the full until the bottom dropped out of his world at lunch-time on a June afternoon in 1938. Due to defend his title in Paisley against Jackie Jurich from California, he failed to make the weight, and became an ex-champion on the scales. They were re-matched at catch-weights in the afternoon. Benny had Jurich down six times before knocking him out in the twelfth. But Benny had blown it, and died in tragic circumstances in 1946, a victim of his own excesses. In the intervening eight years he had become a physical wreck.

British rules do not allow a boxer to be a champion at more than one weight. As soon as he wins a second crown, he must decide which one he is going to retain. This is only fair to other boxers, because while he is waiting to make a title defence in one division, he is automatically blocking another. Divisions that temporarily 'die' are no good for the game.

It is for that same reason that the British Board of Control may declare a domestic title vacant if the holder becomes a world, European, or Commonwealth champion. They do not want the division stagnating. When Ken Buchanan was world lightweight champion and doing most of his fighting in the United States, Jim Watt became British champion, beating Tony Reilly for the vacant title. As soon as Buchanan lost the world title, he was nominated first contender for his old crown and regained it by outpointing Watt.

It seems fair enough to me, even though I once went to war with the Board of Control when we had a deal set up to meet Jimmy Ellis for the vacant world title while Muhammad Ali was having his spot of trouble with the United States Services over his induction to fight in the Vietnam war. Ali was stripped of his title; Ellis and I were matched. There was some question in the States about it being officially recognised, and our Board of Control, instead of backing my claims, went along with the other lot.

That is when I turned in the British title for ten months. With the World Boxing Association and most of the American states supporting Ellis, the Board backed the minority, and I wasn't happy. When I regained the British title, outpointing Jack Bodell at Wembley in 1970, the fight made more money with me as challenger than it would have done had I been champion, because then I would have been defending my title against somebody I'd beaten already. But not getting that Ellis fight was a blow to my pride as well as my pocket.

Incidentally, there are all sorts of ways a boxer can lose his title, other than by being beaten fairly and squarely in the ring or resigning as I did. A British title can go up the wall if a boxer refuses to accept sixty per cent of a purse approved by the Board. In other words, trying to grab too large a slice of the cake can lead to a severe attack of indigestion.

I could also have lost my British title if I had been convicted of a felony or misdemeanour. I should stress that this rule applies only to the British title. The history of boxing in the United States is punctuated with the names of pugs and thugs who have come out of gaol and turned themselves into champions. They are fairly well known, and I'm not going to list the names. Most are better characters for having been in boxing. It has given them something that wasn't there before.

Titles can be forfeited for gross misconduct as a boxer, but generally boxers don't go round clouting folk. Refusal to defend the title after receiving an approved challenge, or being unable to defend for any reason, could cause the Board to declare the title vacant and nominate two others to compete for it.

It depends on the circumstances. The late Jack Solomons once had Bruce Woodcock, the former British heavyweight champion, signed up for a title fight when Bruce had an accident while driving his lorry. The contest was postponed for nearly a year because there was only one reasonable challenger in sight.

British champions are not called upon to defend national titles for six months, though area champions may be called upon after four months. But there again, as in the case of Woodcock, the Board has the power to waive the regulation.

With all due modesty the stewards had to do the same with me, several times. It isn't just a question of running out of opponents. I am not going to be that arrogant. Blokes you have beaten a couple of times will always come up and have another go if the money is right. But that is the whole crux of it. It is no good putting on fights that the public will no longer pay to come and see. If there is no crowd-pulling pretender to the champion's crown, it makes no sense to force him into the ring.

'British is best' certainly applies to the vexed issue of return fights. In the States there have been whole 'series'. Floyd Patterson and Ingemar Johansson fought three times for the world championship. The only way Randolph Turpin could get Sugar Ray Robinson into the ring with him with the world middleweight crown at stake was to promise a return, and Randy was champ for just sixty-four days. But in Britain, return fight clauses are banned. So they should be. It would be very easy, wouldn't it, for two unscrupulous teams of fighters and managers to keep on alternating winning verdicts and, unofficially, splitting the purse monies between them? Meanwhile, other fighters down the line would not get a look in.

The Boxing Board of Control supply Belts for the winners of British titles. They are called Lonsdale Belts – after the fifth earl who was president of the National Sporting Club. They become the property of any fighter who wins a title fight three times, and I am very proud of the fact that I was able to win three of them. No other British boxer has done so well, and it is a feat that cannot be equalled as the Board now rule that no boxer shall receive more than one Lonsdale belt in any one weight division. Theoretically, it would be possible for a fighter to win one at, say, middleweight, light-heavy and then heavy, but in practice, his physique would have filled out long before he could contest a sufficient number of bouts.

My first Lonsdale Belt is in solid gold. The others are silver-plated. Naturally, they are in a safe deposit, for they are extremely valuable. I will leave it to the experts to guess how much, but in one sense, of course, I have to regard them as priceless.

Boxers are no different from ordinary people. They come in all shapes and sizes. Just about the biggest, outside the range of sheer freaks, was Ewart Potgieter, who came to

Britain from South Africa in the early fifties. He was not a gimmick fighter, and had several serious contests. He weighed 23 st 13 lbs, and wasn't quite as quick on his feet as he might have been. We don't really know whether he had a punch or not. It was so long travelling that most opponents saw it well in time to take evasive action.

The heaviest world champion was the Italian, Primo Carnera, who held the title for a year from June 1933. He was 18 st 8 lbs, but though he won the title by knocking out Jack Sharkey in the sixth round, his next two challengers, Paulino Uzcudun and Tommy Loughran, both went fifteen rounds, and when Carnera lost the title to Max Baer, the giant – he stood nearly 6 ft 6 ins – Carnera was in so much distress that the referee had to stop the bout in the eleventh round.

The tallest world champion was Jess Willard, who stood a quarter of an inch higher than Carnera. He became champion in 1915 when he knocked out Jack Johnson in the twenty-sixth round, and didn't defend the title until 1919, when Jack Dempsey fractured Willard's jaw and put him down seven times before he retired after three rounds. Nevertheless, Willard didn't do too badly for a cowboy who didn't start boxing until he was twenty-eight.

That Carnera–Uzcudun set-to might have been one of the least distinguished contests for the world's top boxing honour, but it has its place in the sun. Uzcudun was 16 st $5\frac{1}{4}$ lbs. Carnera weighed in at half a pound below his best fighting weight. Those figures mean that there was an accumulation of 34 st $12\frac{3}{4}$ lbs of men and muscle heaving around the ring. I have never been able to discover whether it took the exhausted referee longer to recover from the clinches than it did the boxers.

And one final mind-boggling performance. Bob Fitzsimmons (12 st 4 lbs) conceded ten stone when he knocked out Ed Dunkhorst (22 st 4 lbs) in 1900. They don't make them like Fitzsimmons any more.

ROUND 11

Money and the Media

As boxing went into the eighties, there was more money in the sport than ever before. Galloping inflation in the seventies ensured that financial records of all description were created annually, but it was the invention of the television satellite that detonated the cash explosion to stratosphere levels.

When Muhammad Ali fought Joe Frazier for the third time – the Thriller in Manila that spilt so much blood before the fight was stopped in the fourteenth round in Ali's favour – he brought his ring earnings, on his own admission, to $29,751,115. As there were more fights to come, including a fitful come-back, I suppose by the time he finished Ali had grossed up something like fifty million dollars.

Traditionally, it is the heavyweights, the big men with the big punches, who pull the crowds and lighten the fans' wallets. Yet nowadays even the smaller men, given charisma and the ability to clout, can command astronomical sums. The Americans, Sugar Ray Leonard and Thomas Hearns, attracted gross receipts of seventeen and a half million pounds when they met for the world welterweight championship at Caesar's Palace, Las Vegas, in September 1981. It seems superfluous to add that it was then the richest fight in boxing history.

Back in 1926, more than 120,000 watched the fight between Jack Dempsey and Gene Tunney and paid $1,895,777. A year later, 104,000 fans handed over $2,658,660 to see the return. By today's standards, they were counting in peanuts.

It was estimated that the Leonard–Hearns drama was seen by 300 million fight fans. The gate at Caesar's Palace was worth three million pounds. Leonard was also involved in the previous record, the £14,000,000 'take' when he clashed with Roberto Duran in July 1980.

There can be no disputing Leonard's right to be regarded as the most exciting boxer of his time, unsurpassed at selling his next fight. Against Hearns, who was unbeaten, Leonard staged one of the most stupendous come-backs. He was so far behind that Hearns must have won had he been able to stay on his feet for the last four minutes and fifteen seconds of the fight. But Leonard finished a fight he looked to have lost with one of the most sustained spells of aggression ever seen in a boxing ring. In the last thirty seconds of the fight, he threw twenty-eight punches at Hearns, and most of them landed, almost all of them hard. The figure of twenty-eight seems almost impossible. How can a man's arms move so fast? But it is true. The fight film was slowed down and the punches were counted. Hearns was in no position to dispute it, but he was eventually able to laugh – all the way to the bank.

International boxing is now ruled by television, at least in the area of finance. No mega-money package can be put together without it. But on local and domestic levels live television coverage clamps an instant brake on the sale of tickets. That is why British promoters will rarely permit screening until some twenty-four hours after the fight.

Like other areas of the entertainment industry, boxing has had to adapt to changing trends and the impact of television. The old fairground booths, once such a marvellous nursery, have almost entirely disappeared, and so too have quite a number of the small-hall shows. I don't think a lot of support has evaporated, but many halls have crumbled before the advance of property development. It was the necessity to change the format that prompted the advent of the dinner shows. Something more than boxing was needed to entice the sporting gentleman away from the small screen.

Yet, despite that, I don't think that boxing can ever recover the losses caused by another form of visual entertainment being available at home, and for free. That is a fact of modern life with which almost every entertainment enterprise has to come to terms. On the theory that they must be joined if they cannot be beaten, promoters of international boxing have learned to work with the boxing authorities and the television companies.

In Britain, the Boxing Board of Control do not negotiate fees with television companies. That is the job of the individual promoter. The Board does not promote. But it doesn't go penniless from television. It collects ten per cent of the fee negotiated between the promoter and the television company, and also takes a proportion from live radio broadcasts.

By common consent, Don King, the Black Muslim who put on so many of Ali's fights, has been the shrewdest of what might be called the international television promoters. Mind you, he had an exciting product to sell, didn't he?

It was King who master-minded the Ali–George Foreman battle in Kinshasa which cost the Zaïre government so many millions. Officially, the bout was part of a music festival, but it was King who hit the right notes. World-wide television is good publicity. The government of Jamaica convinced themselves of that as long ago as 1973, when they did a deal with a television company and backed the world heavyweight title fight between Joe Frazier and George Foreman. Frazier lost his crown when the referee had to stop the contest as early as the second round, but the event put Jamaica's tourist industry on the map.

That was the one that set the gravy-train rolling. Since then, there have been world heavyweight championship fights in such unlikely places as Tokyo, Caracas, Kuala Lumpur, Manila, Puerto Rico, etc. They are hardly bastions of boxing tradition, but the small screen and the mighty dollar rule together.

Television makes some strange demands on fighters, too, because bouts have to be timed to suit the widest audience, and that is usually in the United States. One of Jim Watt's title fights started at two o'clock in the morning. It was a vicious circle. The fight wouldn't have made money at a small venue without television, so if Jim wanted the fight, then two a.m. it had to be. Yet, there is something about boxing in the early hours of the morning that makes it quite an occasion. Which brings me to an important spin-off from the satellite.

Closed-circuit television can be piped into a pay-screen at home or into a cinema. In recent years there has hardly been a space-age satellite promotion that hasn't filled cinemas in London's West End and the bigger population centres in the provinces.

Jarvis Astaire's Viewsport company have become expert at this. Together with the live fight, they will show another from the same bill or screen films of big fights of the past. Either way, the boxing fan gets two or three hours of entertainment for his money.

It is a very sophisticated bargain, and one I am in favour of. The money is channelled back to the principals – the promoter who is risking his cash, and the manager and boxer who are selling their know-how and expertise. Like most professional sportsmen, I believe that offering talent for free, in this case via the home television screen, is not on. Anybody who watches should pay.

I obtained first-hand knowledge of this when I fought Muhammad Ali for the world title. Now that fight took about four months of financial manipulation before it was definitely on. The hiring of Arsenal Stadium was comparatively easy. All we had to do was agree a fee. But the backers of Ali wanted a water-tight guarantee before they would agree to come over. Apart from a title defence against George Chuvalo, of Canada, in Toronto, and previous clash at Wembley, the date at Arsenal was then the only time Ali had fought outside the United States.

At the end of it all, we came to what is a fairly typical arrangement. We worked the contract on a percentage basis, but still with a built-in guarantee. Whichever way the financial ball bounced, we knew we were certain of picking up a minimum figure. Ali, as the champion, asked for a flat guarantee and, quite rightly, got it. On top of that, he had the American and Canadian closed-circuit rights and a percentage on all television, radio and film rights. We had similar rights for Europe and the Far East.

The money is immaterial. After all, I've had it since 1966, and its worth bears no relation to today's cash values. But the breakdown of big-fight finance, even today, will be done largely on those guidelines. You might add a couple of noughts, that's all.

Television should attract sponsorship money into boxing but, frankly, it doesn't. To the uninitiated, this may be rather surprising, but I can explain by asking just one question – where do you put the advertising so that it can't be missed by the television cameras?

If that sounds daft, then think about it. Soccer grounds and cricket grounds, to take just two sports among many, have boards outside the playing area that can be festooned with advertising slogans. Where do you hang them round a ringside?

On the ropes? Fine for the television cameras, but what about the punters in the hall? On the gantry that carries the lights, above the ring? How many times does a television camera poke up there? On the canvas of the ring? Since when did television start transmitting from above the ring? Down one of the corner posts? That's about all. A sponsor can advertise all over the hall, provided the show is not going out on television, but what is the use of that?

Trainers at professional soccer clubs can dash on to the field with their bags proclaiming Spongebest and be certain that they will be seen from every corner of the ground. Who sees the bucket a second carries into a boxing arena?

What about the back of a boxer's dressing-gown, then? Even if television cameras ever do focus on the back of a boxer, and there can't be many less exciting places, any self-respecting director will immediately transmit another shot.

That leaves hardly anything else except the boxer's shorts, and whatever the legend on those, it is hardly legible from beyond the first dozen or so rows.

Even then, television people don't like it. Alan Minter, the former world middleweight champion, once got himself in a hell of a mess when he fought Tony Sibson, from Leicester, and alleviated the pain caused by the loss of his European title by the amount of publicity he generated for Daf, the motor and truck manufacturers.

Minter was a Daf publicist, and was being paid by his sponsors to promote the name of Daf in every direction. When he fought Sibson, the BBC had paid a fee to screen highlights of the fight and interviews, the screening coming the usual twenty-four hours or more after the fight. The BBC had already agreed a fee of something in the region of £50,000 – not bad money, even by 1981 standards. The two boxers would have been expecting to pick up around £15,000 each.

When Minter entered the arena, his four seconds had the magic word Daf on their jackets. When Minter took off his dressing-gown, the balloon went up – because, embroidered on his trunks, was the legend: Daf Trucks.

The decision not to screen the fight was immediate and emphatic. I don't blame Minter for trying. I was sorry for Sibson, though, whose victory – he knocked out Minter in the third round – was the best performance of his career at that stage. How he did it deserved the attention of fight fans everywhere. But I tell the story to underline how difficult it is for boxing to jump on the advertising and sponsorship bandwagon.

Young golfers have been sponsored. A wealthy enthusiast will agree to pay all a promising lad's expenses for a few years in return for, say, twenty-five per cent of his prize-money. That way, in theory, the youngster is freed from financial worries and should be better able to concentrate on his golf. I think it is a fine idea, but if anyone has gambled similarly on a novice boxer, I have yet to hear of it.

In Minter's case, the television authorities were angry because, they claimed, they had been assured that there would be no advertising on his trunks. I am in no position to take sides on that issue, but makers' names have always been prominent on trunks. I used to fight in a new pair of trunks each time, very generously supplied by the London firm of Lonsdale Sports who also looked after any other gear I might require. The fact that television controllers have no objection to that raises yet again the questions of double standards in sports advertising and, regrettably, boxing seems to be one of the sports hardest hit.

Tennis people can play at Wimbledon with advertising and sponsorship identifications easily recognisable on shirt, shorts, racquets . . . in fact on almost anything you care to name.

Racing cars stay in front of the camera lens for minutes on end, and there hasn't been an unadorned speedster since the late Henry Ford was a boy. Athletes like Sebastian Coe and Steve Ovett can be seen, when running in official team events, with a sponsor's name on their vest fronts.

Amateur boxing probably does marginally better than the professionals in the realms of sponsorship. Several firms – Wimpeys the builders are a prime example – will sponsor shows or competitions. Wimpeys, it can be said, make an indirect contribution towards the continuity of professional boxing by underwriting the Amateur Boxing Association championships, and in so doing help to keep the paid ranks supplied with talent.

Radio serves boxing well. It doesn't stop people going to the fights and yet attracts a huge audience when reporting a championship bout. The only danger in radio is that sometimes fights seem better than they actually are. This is simply because the commentator keeps on talking. But he has to. Radio is the one place where silence is not golden.

Boxing has to be grateful, too, for all the newspaper space

it has received over the years, and for its own specialised publications. I am happy to number boxing writers among my best friends.

ROUND 12

Who Rules the World?

Soccer has the Federation of International Football Associations. Cricket has the International Cricket Conference. But no single organisation runs the world of boxing. There is the World Boxing Council, of which the British Boxing Board of Control is a member, and the World Boxing Association.

To anybody outside boxing, the situation must look slightly ridiculous. It would be much tidier to have one ruling body. But, few people in boxing want it. Ours is a cash-motivated game, and the way things are now we can have twice as many world champions, which means twice as many world title fights, which means twice as much money coming in.

There have been attempts to rationalise the position, but they have been mostly no more than half-hearted. There is too much to lose and nothing to win.

The present set-up has its origins in the power game played in the United States. In the first quarter of the century, a body called the New York State Athletic Commission virtually ran world title fights. The Commission was autonomous and autocratic. A few people made a lot of money - and eventually the revolt came. Several states banded together and formed the National Boxing Association, to which, at one time, the British Boxing Board of Control owed allegiance.

Then, in 1963, a number of countries, including Britain, created the World Boxing Council. Without any doubt, it is the premier body. More than a hundred nations belong to it, including several American states.

The move was precipitated by the National Boxing Association's decision in 1962 to call itself the grander-sounding World Boxing Association. It is a confusing situation, but it works. Both organisations recognise each other's disciplinary codes, and it is virtually impossible for any licence-holder, whether he be boxer, promoter, manager or trainer, to work anywhere in the world if he has broken any rules or, in the case of a fighter, if he has failed to get a medical certificate.

Every country has variations on the rules. The use of judges outside the ring to do the scoring is the most glaring example of differences. Another, which we don't use in Britain, is the automatic end to a contest if a boxer is knocked down three times in the same round. But the United States bend this one. They do not apply it in fights for world championships.

The golden rule is that wherever a fighter throws punches, he throws them under local rules or, where titles are at stake, under rules laid down by the appropriate governing body. This system usually works, because referees visit the dressing-rooms before the fight to explain the difference in rules and how he is going to apply them. It doesn't always work, as in that dust-up I had in Rome with Piero Tomasoni, but it does most of the time. Part of the trouble there might have been Tomasoni, but the referee being Dutch didn't seem to help either. I have never really got over him counting when I was gasping for breath and on my knees after being hit by a foul punch in the groin.

European Boxing Union rules, then as now, demand a neutral referee for a title fight, and the principle has since been extended to world fights. Arthur Mercante, a very good American official, has done several in Britain.

Britain can claim to have led the way in boxing administration. The old National Sporting Club was generally accepted as the place for decision-making in the same way that cricket followed the lead of the Marylebone Cricket Club. But just as cricket eventually outgrew the private club for a less autocratic mode of administration, so did boxing.

Promoters, managers and boxers all wanted a more influential say in their own affairs. With the use of bigger halls, they were all making more money than they could out of the National Sporting Club, whose control over the sport gradually waned.

The National Sporting Club did make an attempt to set up a British Boxing Board of Control, but this was largely ineffectual until it was re-constituted in 1929 on a completely independent basis, to become the ruling body we have today.

Nothing is perfect in this world, but I don't see a lot wrong with the way in which boxing is administered. We usually manage to come up with the right answers, and boxers are far less exploited and exposed to danger than they used to be.

ROUND 13

Great Characters of My Time

I was doing one of those sports sessions for charity. The usual question and answer type of thing. Who was the best at this, who was the master of that, what did I think of so and so ... from Muhammad Ali to why I ever started boxing in the first place. I was not in any trouble until a charming lass a few rows from the front landed the proverbial one straight on my jaw.

'What,' she asked, 'do you value most of all the things you've got out of boxing?'

Now there is no easy answer to that. My mind immediately flashed to the obvious, like bank balances, houses, cars and so on. But you can get all those, with some luck, without boxing. What had I got that only boxing could have provided? Then it hit me. The friendship of other boxers.

Ours is a daft game. We spend our working days knocking hell out of each other so that we can become the best of mates. I've been around the boxing scene now for close on forty years, and I've met most of the characters. They are characters, too. Forgive me for being prejudiced, but boxing brings out the best in blokes.

Muhammad Ali, for instance. Forget the public image. He is a sucker for children. When the kids are involved, Ali switches right off. The Greatest, as he likes to refer to himself, silences the loudest noise in boxing. The good deeds are done without the world knowing.

As a fighter, I'm not going to say that Ali was the greatest heavyweight of them all. Personally, I'll put Jack Johnson,

Jack Dempsey, Joe Louis, Rocky Marciano and Ali together at the top of the heap and let them sort it out in the next world. Ali was certainly the fastest of the big men, and had a fighting style that was all his own. But even he would not have been the boxer he was without the shrewd Angelo Dundee behind him.

How shrewd? Well, I have a cutting from the *Philadelphia Inquirer*. It takes the form of an interview with Angelo, who hands out monogrammed cigars to his friends. He was being asked about Cassius Clay's fight with me at Wembley in 1963, and the talk was about the notorious glove incident. Says Angelo:

'They accused me of cutting the gloves. Can you imagine me doing something like that? There was a rip in the gloves. All I did was make the rip a little bigger. They're hunting round for gloves and I'm buying my man time. The way he recuperates, all we need is a couple of minutes.'

But Ali, with children, needs nobody's help. If there is one thing he hated it was to be introduced to the children of any man he had to fight, and I've known him deliberately seek out the offspring of boxers he had battered and have words with them. A strange man, but good company. We usually meet when he is in London.

Ali the non-stop talker was in complete contrast with the much-loved Joe Louis, who did so much for the negro race. The first coloured man to become heavyweight champion of the world for twenty-two years when he knocked out James J. Braddock in 1937, Joe had two favourite words: 'Yep' and 'Nope'.

Conversation with Joe was hard work, especially if anybody wanted to talk about Joe. He died in 1981 after suffering ill-health in his later years, but his fame is eternal. When I watch his old films, it is his style that I so like. It was sheer economy of movement as he shuffled round, always keeping just out of range with the left going jab, jab, jab until he could unleash that fearsome right that put so many opponents away.

When he retired in March 1949, Joe had defended the world title a record twenty-five times, and only three men went the distance with him.

His most bitter fight was against the German, Max Schmeling, the former world champion who knocked out Louis in the twelfth round. It took two years for Louis's handlers to get Schmeling into the same ring as Joe, who had been pleading for the return. Joe took only two minutes and four seconds of the opening round to thrash the German, hitting him so hard with one punch that he was heard to squeal. Schmeling was totally humiliated, and Louis was at last satisfied.

It says everything for boxing that years later when the 'Brown Bomber' ran up a huge bill for hospital treatment, most of it was paid by Schmeling, who had meanwhile become a successful businessman in post-war Germany.

Mums used to bring their babies for Joe to hold, but no such compliment was paid to Jack Dempsey, who held the world heavyweight title from 1919 to 1926. Jack, however, paid me a compliment by coming to the Thomas A'Beckett to watch me train. He must have been getting on a bit then, but he had a sharp fighting brain. One of the all-time greats, he told me how, in his younger days, he was on the point of finishing with the game when a younger brother died. He fixed himself a fight to pay for the funeral expenses.

Dempsey took the title from Jess Willard by knocking him out in the third round. Willard, who was down seven times, said afterwards that he thought the referee was hitting him, too! Some four years later Dempsey, never a man to let an opponent off the hook, met the Argentinian Luis Firpo for the title. It lasted three minutes and fifty-seven seconds, and in that time Firpo had been down nine times, seven of them in the opening round. Dempsey had also been through the ropes, shoved there by the frustrated Firpo.

Jack wasn't the most successful of businessmen when he first retired, but eventually ran a restaurant in New York that became Mecca to every boxing visitor. A terror inside the ring, Jack was a charmer out of it.

Georges Carpentier, who was knocked out in the fourth round when he challenged for Dempsey's world title, was the most notable boxer France ever produced. Although light-heavyweight champion of the world for two years from 1920, he was just not big enough to beat the best of the heavies. Carpentier was another charmer. He was nicknamed the Orchid Man by the ladies, and it stuck. I don't think anybody was surprised when he became the owner of a swish restaurant in Paris.

Georges started fighting professionally when he was fourteen, and his speciality punch was a thumping right hand. He visited Britain regularly until the time of his death and usually made a point of coming to a function organised by Britain's boxing journalists. When I remarked how slim he was for a man well into his seventies, he told me the secret. He still skipped every day, for about twenty minutes.

Carpentier was neatness itself, a trim example of Gallic finesse and the absolute opposite of Rocky Marciano, who is high on my list of men I'm glad I didn't fight. Rocky, an Italian-American, bludgeoned his way to the world heavyweight title in 1952 and retired unbeaten in 1956. He had forty-nine fights, and was taken the full distance only six times.

I met Rocky when he brought his protégé Tony Hughes to London. I found it almost impossible to believe that this quiet, inoffensive man had been such a killer in the ring. Rocky had only one style - to hit, and keep on hitting. His arms would go like pistons, and he had so much confidence, or blind faith, in his own brute strength that he thought nothing of taking three punches to land two.

In civilian clothes, he was short and squat. Stripped for ring action, he looked as powerful as a tank, and such was his style that he would have been disqualified time and time again had he ever fought in Britain or Europe. He gave British champion Don Cockell a world title fight in San Francisco in 1955, knocked him out in the ninth round, and Don was never the same again.

Marciano was so powerful that the force of his punches practically paralysed his opponents' arms. He was oblivious to his own actions when he was in the ring. He hit Cockell with two punches when the Battersea boy was on his knees. When he was asked after the fight why he did it, Marciano couldn't remember delivering the punches and denied that he would do a thing like that. He had to be shown a film of the fight before he was convinced that he had erred.

I don't think any champion could have trained so hard as Rocky. He would leave his family and go up to the mountains for months on end.

Like most Italians, Rocky was a family man, and training got him down in the end. He quit because he wanted to see more of his wife and daughter. Sadly, he was killed in 1969 when his own aircraft crashed.

One of my fighting heroes, when I was a lad, was Jersey Joe Walcott, who won the world heavyweight crown from Ezzard Charles on a seventh-round knock-out in 1951 and lost it to Marciano when he was knocked out in the thirteenth the following year. Joe gave it one more go, was felled in the first round by Marciano, and then wisely decided enough was enough.

What I liked about Joe was that he was in the classical style. He had the perfect physique for a heavyweight. From strong, wide shoulders his body tapered to the thinnest legs it would be possible for a heavyweight to have. He had a good left hook, and actually put Marciano down with it in the opening round of their first fight. That was the first time Rocky had ever been stuck on the canvas.

Jersey Joe earned his glory the hard way. He had been boxing for some twenty years when he became world champion. At thirty-seven, he was the oldest man ever to win it. He later became a boxing referee, and officiated at one of Ali's title fights with Sonny Liston. He was also a lay preacher, and subsequently became mayor of Camden, New Jersey. Jersey Joe is a man of great humility who is a splendid advertisement for the boxing game.

So is Joe Frazier, whose three fights and forty-one rounds with Ali are one of the sagas of boxing. Frazier won the first, to retain his world heavyweight title, in 1971. They clashed again in a twelve-round non-title bout in 1974 which Ali won on points. Then again, for the world crown, in Manila in 1975, when Frazier was stopped in the fourteenth round.

At the end, Smokin' Joe could hardly see. Only his courage kept him upright. And Ali sank to the canvas as soon as he knew he had the verdict. Ali said that a fight like that was the closest thing to dying, and later: 'Joe and I, we've paid all the dues we're ever going to pay each other.'

Frazier was a rough, tough fighter – rather on the lines of Marciano. They both boxed out of a crouch, and an opponent saw only the top of their heads. Like Marciano, he carried an instant sleeping draught in either hand.

In the ring, Frazier was all jungle stuff. Yet he had a very delicate touch when it came to fingering the brass instruments. When he finished with fighting, Smokin' Joe went into show business, touring with his own band. A firm believer in actions speaking louder than words is our Joe. I remember being on the same *This Is Your Life* television programme. There was Joe, who would face any man in the world, rehearsing his lines over and over again, worried stiff.

Surprisingly, Frazier lost his title to George Foreman in 1973, being dumped on the seat of his pants six times inside two rounds. It seemed to suggest that Foreman, then unbeaten in thirty-eight fights, was one of the most fearsome of boxers, but after disposing of Joe Roman in the first round and Ken Norton in the second, Foreman lost out to an ageing Ali in Kinshasa.

Foreman was a very complex character. He started life in the black ghettos of Houston, Texas, married a very young girl, and then refused to fight any more. He said he had had a message from God to pack it up. He joined a religious sect, and has vanished from the public gaze. His was a most odd transformation.

Mean, moody and morose was Foreman, totally unlike Freddie Mills, that lovely buoyant personality who brought the world light-heavyweight championship to Britain in 1948 by outpointing American Gus Lesnevich. Wise-cracking Freddie was the life and soul of every party. He lived in South London, not far from me in Bellingham, and although our careers overlapped only slightly, I saw a lot of him.

Freddie, who was born in Bournemouth, earned his first pay packets as a milkman but supplemented his wages by doing his stuff in a travelling fairground boxing booth. Now that is learning the game the hard way. In 1942 he won the British and Empire light-heavyweight titles by knocking out an elderly Len Harvey, who hadn't fought for three years. Mills finished it in two rounds.

The war and immediate post-war years were hard on Freddie. I have three Lonsdale belts. He never had the chance to win one. For this reason: there were so few light-heavyweights in his time, that he was never called upon to defend his title. Freddie spent most of his time scrapping with heavyweights without ever having the luck to clinch the championship.

After his fighting days were over, Freddie went into show business. It was the early days of television, and Freddie amiably decorated many a show. He also turned boxing promoter, and ran his own night spot in London's West End. It was in a car, outside the same club, that Freddie was found dead, from bullet wounds, in the summer of 1965 at the age of forty-six.

Archie Moore became world light-heavyweight champion by outpointing Joey Maxim in 1952. Nothing startling about that – except that ageless Archie said he was twenty-six at the time, and his mother said he was thirty-nine. Archie came

Before . . . world welterweight champion Sugar Ray Leonard and his son Ray.

After . . . Tommy Hearns hangs out of the ring, having got in the way of a Sugar Ray Leonard punch during their world welterweight title fight.

A boxer just has to face up to it . . . Tommy Hearns takes a left hook from world champion Sugar Ray Leonard.

Chris Finnegan, dumped on the seat of his pants by Bob Foster in their fight for the world light-heavyweight title. Obviously a perfect punch. Finnegan hasn't felt it, and the 'way out' sign in the bottom left of the picture is prophetic.

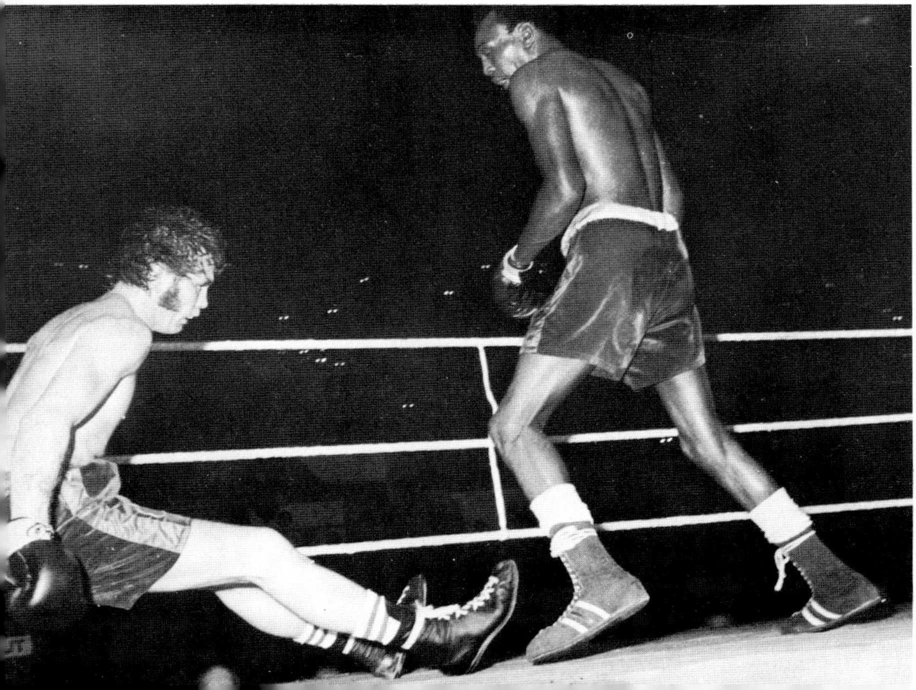

The classical style of Welsh featherweight Howard Winstone, who aims a right at Vincente Saldivar of Mexico during their fight for the world championship in 1967.

Jack Dempsey on the ropes and Gene Tunney on the canvas. If Dempsey had only gone straight to a neutral corner, then Tunney wouldn't have been given the advantage of the long count of fourteen seconds. Tunney always claimed he was in control of the situation, but he might not have recovered inside ten seconds.

Opposite
Publicity sells. Freddie Mills (*left*) and promoter Jack Solomons flank the giant South African Ewart Potgeiter, who was 7 ft 2 ins tall and weighed 23 st 13 lbs.

One of the rare examples of advertising in a boxing ring. Hardly enough to entice big money from potential customers.

Playing the publicity game, with the help of a co-operative opponent, is Freddie Mills, the former British light-heavyweight champion.

OFFICE
FREIGHT CLAIMS AND
ENQUIRIES ETC.
FRENCH
FREIGHT

WORLD CHAMPION AWARD
KAYOED
JOSE NAPOLES
IN
SIX ROUNDS
IN
MEXICO CITY,
MEXICO

Jim Watt (*right*) in action against Howard Davis, of the United States. It was another successful defence of the world lightweight title by Watt, whose six world championship fights are a record by a British boxer.

Opposite: A world championship belt, won by welterweight John H. Stracey, seen here with his wife Michelle.

Bruce Woodcock (*left*), the former British heavyweight champion, exchanges left leads with Freddie Mills. Woodcock preferred the old-fashioned low-cut boots and short socks.

Emile Griffith, the former world middleweight and welterweight champion from the Virgin Islands, demonstrates the art of in-fighting against Harry Scott. Scott wasn't a heavy puncher, and his blows wouldn't travel far enough to hurt Griffith.

from Missouri and was very much his own man. He employed managers, and then made most of the decisions himself. He hung on to the title until 1962, when he was stripped of it. Archie's trouble was that he couldn't resist nipping off to play with the heavies. He had a tilt at Rocky Marciano and got knocked out in the ninth round. Then he chased Floyd Patterson, to whom he must have been giving twenty years, and was stopped in five rounds.

Archie was not a natural light-heavy, and the financial pickings were better in the higher division. But when Archie did have to shed the poundage, he had a unique method, a dream for any weight-watcher. He didn't swallow.

Oh yes, he ate. He chewed, and then removed the food from his mouth so that only the juice went down. Archie's plate, when he had finished a steak, was a fascinating sight. The principle was that no roughage entered the stomach. Me, I'm too fond of my food to try that one, but it must have done something for Archie, who had his last fight in 1963 when he was past fifty. Archie nearly always had a flask. He would never reveal what was in it. An aborigine recipe, he used to say, for keeping strong.

One of nature's gentlemen, Archie went into the entertainment business when he retired, but has since been helping to run youth camps for coloured lads in the United States.

It is dangerous to be dogmatic about boxing records. There are too many gaps in the early years. But it is generally conceded that Archie Moore's feat of winning 141 bouts inside the distance has not been beaten. But that figure is approached by Sugar Ray Robinson, who won 109 of his fights by knock-outs.

Sugar Ray. If ever a boxer had style it was the man who was born in Detroit with the name of Walker Smith. He became Ray Robinson because he did not have a licence when he had his first professional fight and, with typical Sugar smoothness, borrowed one from another boxer.

I think the 1930s, 40s and 50s add up to probably the best

era in boxing. Sugar started in 1940 and finished in 1965. He fought them all and beat them all. He could box. He could punch. And if ever there was a Rolls-Royce among boxers, then it was Sugar Ray Robinson.

His first world title came in 1946, when he beat welterweight Tommy Bell. He defended it five times, successfully of course, before giving it up in February 1951, when he became world middleweight title-holder by knocking out Jake La Motta in the thirteenth round.

There was a hiccup in Sugar's success sequence when he lost the title to Britain's Randolph Turpin in London in July 1951, but he regained it a mere sixty-four days later. Then, in June 1952, the astonishing Robinson tried to take the world light-heavyweight crown from Joey Maxim, but he conceded too much weight and was knocked out in the fourteenth round. That was good enough, said Sugar, and announced his retirement - at thirty-two.

But Sugar couldn't kick the habit. Back he came in 1955, and seven fights later was world middleweight king again after knocking out Bobo Olson in the second round. He lost the title to Gene Fullmer and regained it. He lost it to Carmen Basilio and regained it once more, at the age of thirty-seven. But statistics tell only part of the Robinson legend.

As a showman, he was in the Ali class. When he fought Turpin in London, he had an entourage of seventeen, including his own hairdresser and a golf professional. His boxing robe was a startling pink, and a flamingo-coloured Cadillac ensured that he didn't travel unnoticed. In Paris he caused the traffic to jam in the Champs Elysées, and in London he had to quit the exclusive, expensive Savoy Hotel because his fans were disrupting the running of the hotel.

When, eventually, he quit boxing for good, show business claimed him. He put together a dance routine that typically had taste and toured the night club circuit. Business was good. Everybody wanted to see Sugar. But then he suddenly decided to run a sports foundation for young people in Los Angeles. He had had enough of the sweet life.

Sugar Ray Robinson's mark on boxing is indelible. If ever I started teaching the sport, I would get myself some film of Sugar Ray.

ROUND 14

. . . And More Great Characters

Randolph Turpin, the Leamington Licker, was just twenty-three years old when he outpointed Sugar Ray Robinson in July 1951, to win the world middleweight championship for Britain. It wasn't so much that Randy had won a world title, but that he had beaten the fabulous 'unbeatable' Robinson.

It is difficult to appreciate now, with a dozen or more boxers from Britain having become world champions since, just what an impact that result had. Suddenly, people who had never followed boxing in their lives were aware of Randy Turpin, the ex-Royal Navy cook.

Robinson had been on a European tour. It was said that he wasn't fully fit. It was said that initially he wasn't even considering breaking a holiday for a fight, but British promoter Jack Solomons offered him the sort of money he couldn't refuse, and the match was made. After all, Turpin wasn't expected to cause Sugar Ray too much trouble, although he was British and European middleweight king.

Robinson has always refuted the suggestion that he wasn't fit. He has said: 'I was beaten by a better man who had an unorthodox style.' Robinson has told how he and Joe Louis later cracked the Turpin problem.

'Myself and my friend Joe Louis, the former heavyweight champion, spent hours looking at films of the Turpin fight. Then, one day, Joe spotted something. Turpin had a trick of boxing off the back foot, with his head held back so that he was hard to reach. Louis suggested that I used a feint to get into distance, and Turpin would have to lean so far back that he couldn't stretch any further. Then I could nail him. I did, in the tenth round.'

All that is very complimentary to Turpin, who was certainly our best boxer-fighter of his period. He had a good classical left lead and a big dig in his right hand. But my recollection of the return fight in New York is that Randy had Robinson going again when Randy committed the cardinal sin. He dropped his hands, and Robinson, struggling to last more than another couple of rounds, was in with a big banging right. Though Turpin got up, he continued to take punishment until the referee stopped the contest with eight seconds of the tenth round left.

Turpin was never the same again. When Robinson retired, Turpin was given another chance to win the title but, matched with Bobo Olson, from the United States, he was outpointed over fifteen rounds. From that point on, it was downhill all the way. Randy lost a lot of money trying to turn a castle in Wales into a holiday hotel. He also lost the European title when he was knocked out in the first round by Tiberio Mitri, of Italy. He fought on to become British and Empire light-heavyweight champion, but soon the spark had gone. Turpin died in 1966. Not many of us achieve the impossible dream, but he did.

The next Britisher to become world middleweight champion revelled in it all, and hasn't stopped revelling since. To describe my old mate Terry Downes as colourful is an understatement. He is a human rainbow. He and I have a lot in common, though he gets the decision on cut eyes. He cut worse than I did, though if he nicks himself these days he bleeds pound notes. He has done very well, has our Terry, who enjoys nothing more than being able to refer to his family and their public school education. Not bad for a lad from London's none too salubrious district of Paddington.

Terry took the world middleweight title from America when he stopped Paul Pender in nine rounds in London. Which was a shade ironic because Terry learned his boxing while serving in the United States marines. What happened was that his sister had an accident in the States. Terry's mum went out there to be with her and, subsequently, the whole Downes family followed. Terry spent his teenage years there, joined the United States marines, and won eighty out of eighty-five amateur fights. When he came back to London, his fame had gone on ahead of him and he turned professional with fight manager Jarvis Astaire.

It is not surprising that Terry did well. He loved a fight, the more of a rough and tumble the better. When his business interests started to take off, he could have well afforded to retire from boxing, but he didn't. He did it all quickly. Within a year and a half of joining the paid ranks, he was British champion, and Pender's title came a couple of years later.

Terry was the crashing, bashing sort of fighter who would give 105 per cent. He went back to Pender's home town of Boston for their third meeting, in which Pender took a points decision. After a few more fights and a bust-up with the British Board of Control which resulted in his losing the British title, the intrepid Terry had one more crack at world honours. He let a little extra poundage creep on and faced Willie Pastrano for the world light-heavyweight title at Manchester. Willie, an extremely clever boxer, knew a little too much for our lad. Terry had enough savvy to call his book *My Bleeding Business*, and retire.

He had a share in a chain of betting-shops, became a property tycoon when the old Hurst Park racecourse was developed, and now does as he likes, I think. When he finds the need for a little action, he does some work as a film extra. Terry is one of those larger-than-life extrovert characters.

The old timers will always have it that British boxing will never produce a finer welterweight than Ted 'Kid' Lewis, who won the world championship in 1915 and kept it, on and off, until 1921. A Jew from London's East End, he was the first British champion to win a world title in the United States – in fact the only one until Ken Buchanan equalled the feat.

'Kid' Lewis came up the hard way and was never anything else but a professional boxer. He started at fifteen and, over a career of twenty years, collected titles like confetti. Apart from the world crown, Lewis won three European, two Empire and three British titles.

Lewis was so popular in the United States that it is reckoned that he made more than £150,000 over there, to lift his career income to something in the region of £250,000, a colossal sum in those days. The foundation of the Kid's fortunes was the longest-running boxing series of them all. The Kid and Jack Britton, an Irish-American, fought twenty times, of which Britton won four and Lewis three, with one being drawn and twelve being no-decision contests.

The background to no-decision contests is that they were a device used in the United States at that time to 'legalise' boxing. Not all the States adopted the law which decreed that boxing must be confined to members of bona fide clubs, the rounds restricted to ten and no result given at the end of the bout. But bets were struck on fights and the judgement given by newspaper reporters at the ringside.

Ted was a great-hearted character. He lived by the creed that money was to be enjoyed, and as he started life without any and couldn't take it with him, it was used to the full. He lived, when the big money was coming in, at a rate of a thousand pounds a week. But he thought nothing of paying to take a thousand schoolchildren to the seaside for a day to celebrate one of his victories.

I have a great admiration for Ted, who died in 1970. He went over there, took on the Yanks and beat them at their own game. He left Britain as a stylish boxer, and came back as a fighter who could slug it out with anybody. He was revered in London's East End. Even men of substance always raised their hats to the Kid.

One of Lewis's successors as world welterweight champion was Emile Griffith, a Virgin Islander who came over to London twice in 1964, to retain his world title by outpointing

Brian Curvis of Wales, and then knocking out Dave Charnley, one of our best post-war boxers, in nine rounds.

Griffith, a fine technician with a spark of venom, made more comebacks than a boomerang. Twice he regained the welterweight prize, and when he moved up to middleweight, that title was won, lost, won and lost again.

There haven't been many real grudge fights in boxing, at least not in my experience, but Griffith was concerned in one of them. Back in 1961, Griffith fought Benny Paret of Cuba for the world welterweight title and won it with a thirteenth-round knock-out. Six months later, Paret retrieved his title on a split verdict that made a third fight a natural. This was arranged, six months later, in March 1962, but somewhere along the line, Paret made his fatal mistake. He cast doubts on Griffith's masculinity – not realising that the Virgin Islander could understand Spanish. An angry Griffith finished the fight in the twelfth round with Paret caught on the ropes. The official fight film shows that Paret took twenty-one blows during the last assault. Paret was unconscious for ten days before he died in hospital, but to be fair to referee Ruby Goldstein, there had been no sign of serious injury before Paret's collapse.

Tommy Farr must have done more for British boxing prestige than any other man who failed to win a world title. To go the distance with Joe Louis when the 'Brown Bomber' was at his peak is one of the stories we will hand down the generations. Like Freddie Mills, Tommy Farr came from the boxing booths, and has told me time and again what a struggle he had to become recognised. He badly wanted a crack at Jack Petersen's British heavyweight title, but was continually sidestepped. He eventually won the title, by outpointing Ben Foord, Petersen's successor, but his past battles with the Board no doubt influenced his decision to stay on in the United States and have other fights instead of coming home. So the Board fined Tommy, stripped him of his title and suspended him. Shades of my spot of bother some thirty years later!

Farr was Louis's first title defence. The Americans thought they had signed up a soft-touch Limey. But just to illustrate how hard they play it over there, they called Tommy to the ringside twenty minutes before the bout was due to start! Imagine, the fight of your life, and you are stuck out there, nerves on edge, watching a preliminary contest. This, as I see it, makes Farr's tremendous achievement that much greater.

Farr's successor as British champion was Len Harvey, one of the most popular of British boxers, who, though he was a natural light-heavy, twice won the heavyweight title.

Len's big handicap was lack of a real punch. He was a clever fighter, a spoiling fighter who knew too much for most of his opponents. He might even have been a world champion. Just before the outbreak of war, on 10 July 1939, Harvey outpointed Jock McAvoy, a tough Lancastrian, for what the British Boxing Board of Control were prepared to recognise as the vacant world light-heavy championship. Nice try, but there isn't an American book of boxing records that doesn't have John Henry Lewis resigning his title to fight as a heavyweight, and Billy Conn, who twice went in with Joe Louis for the world heavyweight crown, becoming the light-heavyweight champion by outpointing Melio Bettina on 25 September.

My dad saw Len fight a couple of times at the old Blackfriars Ring where Jim Wicks did a job as Number 2 to Dan Sullivan, the promoter. Harvey was every schoolboy's hero in the thirties, and had the astonishing record of having been knocked out only once in 418 professional contests.

That was his last, in 1942, when he was persuaded, against his better judgement, to put his British and Empire light-heavyweight titles at stake against the young Freddie Mills at Tottenham football ground. No man goes 417 fights without taking the full count unless he has exceptional boxing ability. But Len had been out of the ring nearly three years. He was thirty-five. Mills needed less than two rounds. A right sent Len through the ropes and he was counted out, standing on his feet, but still outside the ring.

I think George and I might be a bit unusual. There are not many twins who become professional boxers, and not many brothers who both become champions. Two of the rare ones, in more senses than one, are the Finnegans, Chris and Kevin. Chris was British light-heavyweight champion in 1971–73 and Kevin was top middleweight in 1974, and again in 1977 and 1979 when Alan Minter went off in search of the world title. Chris, too, got a second bite at the light-heavyweight honour when John Conteh was concentrating on world events. Both Chris and Kevin won Lonsdale belts, which is a family feat that will take some beating.

The Finnegans came from good Irish stock, and can do their share of hell-raising. Chris was probably the better boxer of the two. He won Olympic gold in Mexico in 1968 and earned himself a shot at Bob Foster's world light-heavyweight crown. Foster, a very fierce puncher from the United States, defended his title fourteen times, and Finnegan did better than most in lasting to the fourteenth round.

Maurice Hope, who won the world light-middleweight title for the Terry Lawless stable when he outpointed Rocky Mattioli in San Remo in 1979, is an unlucky fighter. He never received the acclaim he deserved. Born in Antigua, but reared in Hackney, he is a man of few words and strong character. Not many would have the courage to come back to boxing after having an operation on a detached retina, but Maurice did. Nobody wins a world title without having to do some battling, but Maurice is one of these professionals who goes out there and does a job without fuss.

Maurice could never, for instance, be another Eric Boon, that cracking lightweight from Cambridgeshire who set British boxing aflame just before the 1939 war. Eric was one of those people to whom things happen. He was still thirteen days away from his nineteenth birthday when he became champion by knocking over Dave Crowley. 'Boy' Boon had arrived. Less than a year later, before he had even left his teens, he won a Lonsdale belt.

His classic contest was with Arthur Danahar, from Bethnal Green, which became the first British fight to be televised on closed-circuit to cinemas – and that was back in 1939. The war came at the wrong time for Eric, but he had the sort of following that Maurice Hope, among others, would have envied.

Eric was always on the brink of making a fortune. One of his great ideas was pneumatic gloves. I never did find out how the air was supposed to stay in. Another time, he had a load of fight films which he was taking round the clubs and showing as part of the evening's entertainment. More often than not, something would go wrong with the spools. Whenever I saw Eric, he always seemed to have most of the film on the floor.

Britain's lightweights have done us proud in recent years. Dave Charnley, from Dartford, twice fought Joe Brown for the world title, in 1959 and 1961; Ken Buchanan won it; and then Jim Watt followed suit.

Jim Watt has done well – so well that I hope he never reconsiders his decision to retire. I don't think it likely. He has a good business head, and if the garage starts to lose money, Jim can always get a crust as an entertainer. He is a good speaker, and tells good gags.

Watt worked hard for what he achieved, but I doubt whether any British boxer has put in more heart-breaking graft before becoming a world champion than Howard Winstone, the featherweight from Merthyr Tydfil. Winstone took the British title from Terry Spinks in 1961, eventually retiring undefeated after nearly eight years. In 1963 he was European champion following his defeat of Alberto Serti. In 1965 came the great chance. Winstone faced world champion Vicente Saldivar in London – and lost on points. They met again at Cardiff. Once more Winstone went the whole way, and once more he was outpointed. There was a third meeting, in Mexico City, where Winstone received a pasting, the fight being stopped in the twelfth.

But Saldivar had had enough. He retired after that fight, and Winstone was matched with Mitsunori Seki of Japan in London, and at long, long last, Winstone was crowned. The fight was stopped in his favour in the ninth round. But within six months, the title was gone. José Legra of Spain stopped Winstone in five rounds in front of a shocked Welsh audience at Porthcawl.

Winstone was a brilliant boxer. It is a shame that Wales so rarely produces any *fighters*.

It certainly couldn't have been Winstone – or any of the fighters I've talked about in these last two chapters – involved in the classic I heard the last time I went to Shoreditch Town Hall, one of London's last small-hall venues.

Frankly, the fight wasn't very good. The lads were doing their best, but, in truth, they were messing each other about.

Finally, from one side of the hall, came the cry: 'Turn the light out, I want to go to sleep.' And from the other side: 'Don't do that, I'm trying to read.'

With humour like that, boxing can survive.

ROUND 15

The Rules of Boxing

(as laid down by the British Boxing Board of Control)

1 Contests All Contests to be decided in a three-roped ring with the ropes joined in the centre at each side, not less than 16 feet or more than 20 feet square and not less than 18 inches margin of ring floor outside the ropes. The floor must be covered with canvas over a safety mat approved by the Board. Corner posts to be padded.

Boxers must shake hands before the commencement of the Contest and at the beginning of the final round, and must defend themselves at all times.

2 Dress and Bandages Contestants must be stripped to the waist, box in Regulation boots without heels or spikes, with Regulation shorts.

The gloves to be of a weight of 6 ounces each for Flyweights to Light-Middleweights and 8 ounces each for Middleweights to Heavyweights. (Breaking by twisting, removal of padding by fingering and thumbing from the potential part of the glove is prohibited.) Contestants to weigh on the day of the Contest.

Bandages are permitted for the protection of the hands. If used, they must not exceed 18 feet of 2 inch soft bandage for all weights, and/or 9 feet of 1 inch Zinc Oxide plaster tape for weights up to and including Middleweights, and 11 feet of 1 inch Zinc Oxide plaster tape for Light-heavy and Heavyweights. In all cases, these lengths are for each hand. The tape must not be applied over the knuckles.

3 Officials In all Contests, a Referee must officiate inside the Ring and a Timekeeper shall be appointed.

In all Contests no more than four persons acting as a Second shall be allowed in each corner.

The Seconds shall leave the Ring when ordered to by the Timekeeper; the Referee to see this is carried out.

The Seconds shall give no advice or assistance to the Contestants during the progress of any round.

4 Medical examination and number of rounds Contestants shall be medically examined immediately after the weigh-in on the date of the Contests.

In all Contests the number of rounds shall be specified. No Contest shall exceed 15 rounds nor be of less than 12 minutes' duration; except in the case of novice competitions which may be of eight minutes' duration. Rounds shall be of three minutes' duration, except in Contests of ten rounds and under when rounds may be of two minutes' duration.

The interval between rounds shall be one minute.

5 Referee's Marking The Referee shall award a maximum number of ten marks at the end of each round to the better man and a proportionate number to the other Contestant or, when equal, the maximum number to each.

Marks shall be awarded for 'attack' – direct clean hits with the knuckle part of the glove of either hand or any part of the front or sides of the head, or body above the belt (the belt is an imaginary line drawn across the body from the top of the hip bones); 'defence' – guarding, slipping, ducking or getting away. Where Contestants are otherwise equal, the majority of marks shall be given to the one who does most part of the leading off or who displays the better style.

If a Contestant is down he must get up unassisted within ten seconds; his opponent meanwhile shall retire to the farthest neutral corner and shall not resume boxing until ordered to do so by the Referee. A man is considered down even when he is on one foot or both feet, if at the same time any other part of his body is touching the ground, or when he is in the act of rising. A Contestant failing to continue the Contest at the expiration of ten seconds shall not be awarded any marks for that round, and the Contest shall then terminate.

In the event of the count being interrupted by the bell signifying the end of the round, the Contest and count shall continue, either until the Boxer who is down rises, or until the 'out' is reached, in which case the Contest shall terminate.

The count shall not continue when the bell signifies the termination of the final round of the Contest.

If at the conclusion of any round during the Contest one of the Contestants should attain such a lead on points as to render it an impossibility for his opponent to win, he must then be declared the winner.

The referee shall decide each Contest in favour of the Contestant who obtains the greater number of marks.

(a) When ordered by the Referee to 'break', both Boxers shall immediately take one step back before re-commencing to box. A Boxer shall not strike or attempt to strike his opponent on the 'break'.

At the end of each Contest, which lasts the scheduled number of rounds, the M.C. shall announce the Referee's final score.

6 Disqualification The Referee shall have power to disqualify a Contestant for any of the following acts: (a) hitting below the belt; (b) using the 'pivot blow'; (c) hitting on the back of the head or neck; (d) kidney punching; (e) hitting with the open glove, the inside or butt of the hand, or with the wrist or elbow; (f) holding, butting or careless use of the head, shouldering, wrestling, roughing; (g) not trying; (h) persistently ducking below the waist-line; (i) intentional falling without receiving a blow; (j) failing to break when so ordered, or striking or attempting to strike an opponent on the break; (k) deliberately striking an opponent when he is dropping to the floor or is down; (l) ungentlemanly conduct; (m) any other act or conduct which he may deem foul.

A Contestant disqualified for any cause whatever shall not be entitled to any prize or remuneration, except in accordance with Regulation 20, para 15 (which allows the money to be distributed among the promoter, manager, trainer, sparring partner or partners and the boxer himself at the discretion of the appropriate disciplinary authorities).

7 Referee's Power The Referee shall have power to stop the Contest if, in his opinion, a contestant is outclassed or accidentally disabled.

8 Discretion The Referee shall decide (1) any question not provided for in these Rules; (2) the interpretation of any of these Rules on matters arising during the time the Contestants are in the Ring.

9 Referee's Decision The Referee's decision shall be final.